T0383087

Public Policy and the Impact of COVID-19 in Europe

This book analyses Europe's COVID-19 response provided by governments and societies, to assess its influence on the economy from both short- and long-term perspectives.

The authors argue that there are three key factors that determine how successful a given country is. The first is the determination and effectiveness of the government. The second is the capacity of states and their healthcare systems in times of crisis. The third is society's willingness to adhere to emergency measures and to cooperate with authorities. The book examines the government policy of EU states during the pandemic, studies the behaviour of EU societies, reveals the influence of the pandemic crisis on the economy of EU states, and formulates a successful strategy to counteract the challenges wrought by the pandemic.

The book will appeal to scholars and researchers engaged in the fields of economic and political science, global studies, and international relations. Furthermore, it will also be addressed to policy-makers of European States as it contains a complex analysis of their policy responses and the corresponding impact on European economy and society.

Magdalena Tomala is Associate Professor in the Department of Law and Social Sciences, Jan Kochanowski University, Kielce, Poland.

Maryana Prokop is Assistant Professor at the Institute of International Relations and Public Policies, Jan Kochanowski University, Kielce, Poland.

Aleksandra Kordonska is Assistant Professor at the Higher School of Public Administration in Kielce, Poland, and a lecturer at the Institute of Political Science, Warmia and Mazury University, Olsztyn, Poland.

Routledge Focus on Economics and Finance

The fields of economics are constantly expanding and evolving. This growth presents challenges for readers trying to keep up with the latest important insights. Routledge Focus on Economics and Finance presents short books on the latest big topics, linking in with the most cutting-edge economics research.

Individually, each title in the series provides coverage of a key academic topic, whilst, collectively, the series forms a comprehensive collection across the whole spectrum of economics.

Islamic Economics and COVID-19
The Economic, Social and Scientific Consequences of a Global Pandemic
Masudul Alam Choudhury

The Economics of Intellectual Property and Openness
The Tragedy of Intangible Abundance
Bartłomiej Biga

Economics, Education and Youth Entrepreneurship
International Perspectives
Marian Noga and Andrzej Brzeziński

Markets vs Public Health Systems
Perspectives from the Austrian School of Economics
Łukasz Jasiński

Public Policy and the Impact of COVID-19 in Europe
Economic, Political and Social Dimensions
Magdalena Tomala, Maryana Prokop and Aleksandra Kordonska

For more information about this series, please visit: www.routledge.com/ Routledge-Focus-on-Economics-and-Finance/book-series/RFEF

Public Policy and the Impact of COVID-19 in Europe

Economic, Political and Social Dimensions

**Magdalena Tomala,
Maryana Prokop,
and Aleksandra Kordonska**

Routledge
Taylor & Francis Group

LONDON AND NEW YORK

First published 2022
by Routledge
4 Park Square, Milton Park, Abingdon, Oxon OX14 4RN

and by Routledge
605 Third Avenue, New York, NY 10158

Routledge is an imprint of the Taylor & Francis Group, an informa business

© 2022 Magdalena Tomala, Maryana Prokop and Aleksandra Kordonska

The right of Magdalena Tomala, Maryana Prokop and Aleksandra Kordonska to be identified as authors of this work has been asserted in accordance with sections 77 and 78 of the Copyright, Designs and Patents Act 1988.

All rights reserved. No part of this book may be reprinted or reproduced or utilised in any form or by any electronic, mechanical, or other means, now known or hereafter invented, including photocopying and recording, or in any information storage or retrieval system, without permission in writing from the publishers.

Trademark notice: Product or corporate names may be trademarks or registered trademarks, and are used only for identification and explanation without intent to infringe.

British Library Cataloguing-in-Publication Data
A catalogue record for this book is available from the British Library

Library of Congress Cataloging-in-Publication Data
A catalog record for this book has been requested

ISBN: 978-1-032-11989-2 (hbk)
ISBN: 978-1-032-11993-9 (pbk)
ISBN: 978-1-003-22253-8 (ebk)

DOI: 10.4324/9781003222538

Typeset in Times New Roman
by Apex CoVantage, LLC

Contents

Figures

Tables

Preface

An outbreak of the Coronavirus Disease 2019 (COVID-19), which has been spreading globally and is defined as a pandemic in recent times, became a serious challenge for people, governments, and economies all over the world. Considering such priorities today as saving human life and reducing the spread of virus, governments also seek ways to provide an effective policy in different spheres of social, economic, and political life. The success in times of crisis could be ensured on the basis of the cooperation of national authorities with societies and experts in various fields, the possibility of a quick response to problems, the effective process of exchange of information, forecast, and developing of strategies to counteract the challenges. The second wave of coronavirus in the European Union (hereafter: EU) confirms that states were unprepared for the pandemic. Therefore, the main purpose of our work was to analyse Europe's COVID-19 response provided by governments and societies and to assess its influence on the economy in short- and long-term perspectives.

The book is innovative in its nature because it contains a scientific investigation on how EU States cope with such a huge and current challenge as the coronavirus pandemic. Taking into account the fact that pandemic is a new phenomenon in modern history, there are no verified methods or appropriate strategies which could be applied by authorities. European States are just in the process of studying how to counteract this challenge. So, in view of the outbreak, which has been spreading since the end of 2019, today we have an opportunity to assess the governments' response, to analyse the behaviour of societies and to study the impact of all actions on the economy of European States. Authors' original thought was to apply an interdisciplinary approach with the aim to present a complex investigation through the prism of global studies, to make conclusions and formulate recommendations for policy-makers and governing bodies.

The current pandemic crisis shows that neither political nor economic relations should be a focal point in international relations, but humans, and their health and life. The politics, focusing on gaining voters' support, should be relegated to the background, while effective state management should be in the foreground. Governments need to set aside their political leniencies and follow the recommendations of experts and other technocrats; they must act early and swiftly; and they should be efficient in making working trade-offs with the society, economic interest groups, and even the political opposition. There are three key factors that determine how successful the country is. The first one is the determination and effectiveness of the government. The second one is the capacity of states and their healthcare systems in times of crisis. The third one is the society's willingness to adhere to emergency rules and to cooperate with authorities. Thus, our main objectives are:

- to analyse the government policy of the EU states in times of pandemic;
- to study the behaviour of the EU societies;
- to reveal the influence of the pandemic crisis on the economy of EU states and to define whether the European economy can survive the crisis.

The main hypothesis of the work is that cooperation of policy-makers and society is the most effective way to deal with a pandemic crisis in all dimensions.

Chapter 1 of the book contains an analysis of COVID-19 response of EU Member States from both legal and political perspectives in the context of preventing and counteracting the coronavirus pandemic based on Governments' Policy COVID Index. The study covers two waves of spreading: the first one is in spring 2020 and the second one is in autumn 2020. Obtained results enabled to define whether Member States have implemented a uniform policy within the EU (i.e. have used similar mechanisms and instruments) and which countries have applied the most restrictive/liberal catalogue of measures in fight against a pandemic.

Chapter 2 contains an analysis of attempts made by European societies towards the spreading of coronavirus. At the beginning, we discussed the social capital according to the newest literature. The focus is put on such factors as respect for common values and collective action in societies. According to Pierre Bourdieu and Francis Fukuyama's ideas, we tried to evaluate a correlation between social capital and people's behaviour in the era of coronavirus. Thus, the study enables us to distinguish the States, which are the most and the least effective from the perspective of social capital. The third part of the chapter contains an analysis of the social responsibility aimed at presenting how the societies behave under new rules and restrictions applied for suppressing the epidemic in different States.

The main goal of Chapter 3 was to assess the influence of the pandemic crisis on the economy of EU states and to define whether the European economy can survive the crisis. This chapter aimed to address the following key questions: What is the impact of COVID-19 on the EU economy and how is the impact distributed among different sectors? How comprehensive are the recovery measures and to what extent they are meeting the needs of the EU? Whether the economic support has been provided in accordance with changes in the level of restrictions? What is the proper policy response to problematic long-term economic trends? The first part of the chapter contains an overall analysis of the economic effects of COVID-19 in EU countries based on main economic indicators. The second part reveals the impact of COVID-19 on EU industries. The next part highlights the assessment of the COVID-19 response of the EU countries by using Pearson correlation to define the relationship between the level of restrictions, economic support, and confidence in the economy of the EU citizens. The last part presents a long-term perspective of the pandemic in the EU countries as well as the key recommendations on the recovery measures and policies.

Our intended audience is first of all scholars and academic staff. Considering the interdisciplinary approach of our work, we assume that it could be useful for those engaged in the field of global studies, international relations, political, and economic science. Furthermore, it is also addressed to policy makers of European States, as it contains a complex analysis of the EU policy, its impact on European societies and economy with some recommendations.

1 Policy response to coronavirus in European member states

Maryana Prokop

Introduction

The onset of the SARS-CoV-2 virus dated to the end of December 2019, when an unknown respiratory disease was identified in Wuhan, the capital of China's Hubei Province, and the virus was commonly referred to as COVID-19. The spread of the COVID-19 epidemic worldwide and its growth to the scope of a pandemic undoubtedly became a major challenge for European countries in the way of protecting the lives and health of their citizens and working to avoid destabilising state economies as a result of the applied restrictions. The main problem in all countries affected by the virus was the limited capacity of health systems, and above all, the lack of knowledge about the threat, which hindered the selection of measures and tools to prevent, combat, and mitigate the effects of the pandemic. Each of the EU Member States sought its own solutions to the pandemic and acted on the new situation to guarantee national stability at the political, social, and economic levels. A number of restrictions that were proposed and implemented by the governments of the Member States were a significant challenge to their search for effective solutions to the situation (based on the recommendations of the World Health Organization [WHO]). The applied restrictions have become known as lockdown, which translates into the terms "isolation," "quarantine," "prohibition" and "injunction." The restrictions adopted by the states oscillated around restricting mobility and reducing population centres by limiting flights, closing schools and educational institutions, sports and recreational facilities, and places of public use, as well as in the most extreme cases, banning the movement of people (WHO, 2021). However, the manner of implementation and the scope of introduced restrictions were defined by each country in its own way through adapting to its own needs and the course of the pandemic in a given country. For the purposes of this part of the chapter, state actions (restrictions) are referred to as "covidian" policy.

DOI: 10.4324/9781003222538-1

The global epidemic threat has led to a redefinition of the meaning of the role of health care and health policy in the context of state security policy-making. The aim of this part of the study was to analyse policy response to coronavirus in European Member States. Addressing the research problem of this part of the work, the following questions were posed: What tools were used in member states to prevent the spread of the COVID-19 pandemic? Were the actions of EU governments more radical or liberal in nature? Were the "covidian" policies of EU countries consistent or individual in nature? The main problem was considered to be the question [Q]: To what extent did the "covidian" policies of the countries have an individual character, and to what extent were the EU countries based on a common catalogue of solutions? For the research problem, the main hypothesis was formulated taking into account that the threat of COVID-19 was a new phenomenon and each country had to develop instruments to combat it on its own. The main hypothesis was adopted as the statement, [H], that the "covidian" policy of EU countries to a large extent had an individual character, through individual search for solutions by individual Member States depending on the epidemiological situation in a given country. The working hypothesis [H_0] was also applied – that the policy of EU countries to a large extent had a common character, through the application of similar solutions.

1.1   Methodological assumptions

Our world in data, the World Bank database, the Response Measures Database, and the websites of the Ministry of Health and the Ministries of Foreign Affairs of the European Union Member States (Austria, Belgium, Bulgaria, Croatia, Cyprus, the Czech Republic, Denmark, Estonia, Finland, France, Germany, Great Britain,[1] Greece, Hungary, Ireland, Italy, Latvia, Lithuania, Luxembourg, Malta, the Netherlands, Poland, Portugal, Romania, Slovakia, Slovenia, Spain, and Sweden), as well as of the most important organisations, institutions, and agencies, both national and international, responsible for public health (e.g. WHO) were researched to find pertinent information. As a research method, content analysis has been applied to collect and group information in the context of the effectiveness of actions applied by EU governments to combat the COVID-19 pandemic.

First, the aim of this part of the work was to construct a research tool that would make it possible to determine to what extent the actions of EU governments were effective under the circumstances and brought about a reduction in the number of cases and deaths from COVID-19. The analysis and aggregation of solutions applied by the EU countries (introduced restrictions) in the face of the epidemiological threat significantly revised the manner of conducting research and the assumptions that the authors made at the preparatory stage of the monograph.[2] Governments Policy COVID Index [GPCI] was used as a research tool. The study included the reference to the EU countries' applied actions (restrictions) in the fight against the pandemic using the GPCI index, created to verify the research problem of this part of the publication.

To create the GPCI, the assumption of EU countries' policies to combat and prevent the spread of the COVID-19 pandemic was used. To date, the leading research on how governments respond to a pandemic has been conducted as part of the Oxford COVID-19 Government Response Tracker project (Hale, T., Anania. J., Angrist., N., & all. (2021)). Researchers conducted an analysis based on 11 indicators of government response and created the Government Response Stringency Index (Stringency Index), which allows for effective international comparisons of government interventions. For the Stringency Index, the following aspects were considered: school closures, workplace closures, cancellation of public events, restrictions on public gatherings, closures of public transportation, stay-at-home requirements, public information campaigns, restrictions on internal movements, and international travel controls. In contrast, the Oxford Coronavirus Government Response Tracker made use of 23 indicators: containment and closure (school closing, workplace closing, cancellation of public events, restrictions on gathering size, closing public transport, staying at home requirements, restrictions on internal movement, and restrictions on international travel); economic response (income support, debt/contract relief for households, fiscal measures, and giving international support); health system (public information campaign, testing policy, contact tracing, emergency investment in healthcare, investment in COVID-19 vaccines, protection of elderly people, vaccination policy, and facial coverings); vaccine policy (vaccine prioritisation, vaccine eligibility/availability, and vaccine financial support); and the miscellaneous (other responses) (Hale et al., 2021, p. 5).

In turn, the Response Measures Databases (RMD) of the European Centre for Disease Prevention and Control (ECDD) and the Joint Research Centre (JCR) of the European Commission are a regularly updated archive of non-pharmaceutical interventions introduced in 30 countries in EU and European Economic Area (EEA) in response to the COVID-19. Measurements are recorded according to a three-level hierarchical coding system (levels 1, 2, and 3). Level 1 includes measurements of the following activities:

(1) Physical distance, which is the broadest category of measures, including measures aimed at limiting contact between persons, closing public transport, and closing educational institutions. (2) Hygiene and safety measures refer to measures to reduce the infectiousness of contacts (e.g. use of protective masks) and measures concerning disinfection of public spaces. (3) Case management and quarantine: this corresponds to interventions

related to COVID-19 case management and contacts. (4) Ensuring access to treatment. (5) General measures: public information, risk assessment, or activation of crisis management teams. (6) Hygiene and safety measures: this includes measures to reduce the infectiousness of contacts (e.g. use of protective masks) and measures concerning disinfection of public spaces. (7) Internal travel: this refers to all measures restricting travel and mobility within a country. (8) International travel: collects measures that restrict international travel (e.g. movement across borders and closure of international borders) (The Response Measures Database, n.d.).

Similar to the Stringency Index [SI] for determining the intensity of restrictions implemented by countries, the GPCI takes into account the intensity of restrictions implemented by assigning weight to specific measures. However, the GPCI was used as a tool to determine whether EU "covidian" restrictions were common or individual to each country. The Response Measures Database, on the other hand, has a much broader dimension, as it not only focuses on issues related to the introduction of restrictions but also examines the data of restrictions applied in a three-level hierarchy of measurement. The operationalisation of the Government Policy COVID Index was based on the analysis of the policy of action of Member States in terms of a catalogue of actions/restrictions/recommendations to prevent the spread of pandemics in relation to the effects of their introduction in terms of effectiveness. The analysis of the actions applied by governments in the EU made it possible to extract the following X_{1-9}[3] variables for the GPCI:

[X_1] – emergency legal measures;

[X_2] – mask covering;

[X_3] – distance learning (e-learning) – including closure of educational institutions: kindergartens, schools, and universities;

[X_4] – remote working (restrictions and recommendations on online working and sanitation at work);

[X_5] – travel, introduction of restrictions on entry into other countries (bans, requiring tests or confirmation of vaccination); international movement restrictions;

[X_6] – restrictions on movement within own state: limitations imposed on sports and cultural facilities, public gatherings, and social meetings;

[X_7] – closing of stores, except for stores securing the most important needs (introduction of capacity limits and ordering wearing masks within stores);

[X_8] – catering and events, ban on mass events, and closure of catering facilities (takeaway orders); and

[X_9] – public transport restrictions.

The analysis of the variety of restrictions undertaken in the EU countries allowed for their typologisation into "strong" and "low-strength" ones. In order to determine whether the actions of the rulers of EU states, in the context of the intensity of restrictions, were radical (strong) or liberal (weak), a gradation into: radical (strong) – "Strength" [S] – assuming that the given actions have the character of restrictions, orders, and prohibitions, and for non-compliance with them the natural and/or legal person bears the consequences (e.g. fine), and liberal (weak) defined as "Low Strength" [L] – having the character of recommendations and proposals. It is worth noting that certain actions may have a more liberal character in one country (e.g. applied as recommendations), while in another one, a given solution will be an order (and failure to comply will result in legal consequences). Therefore, a given gradation may have deviations in individual cases. In addition, the determination of the radicality of the introduced restrictions may have a variable character, in relation to the stages (waves) of the course of the pandemic, which may result in the loosening or tightening of restrictions. In this case, in a given study, the actions of governments in the stages of the increasing trend of morbidity were taken into account, in order to verify their highest power (restrictiveness).

The selection and determination of the restrictive or permissive degree of the applied actions in the "covidian" policy of the EU countries or the lack of it in relation to the introduced actions by the EU Member States may be charged with subjectivity. The authors, while undertaking this task, were fully aware of this danger and the appearance of a margin of error in assessing the policy of countries in this area.

1.1.1 Establishing the scale for the GPCI

The first step involves operationalising the variables for the established indicators X – defining the actions of the government in the context of restrictiveness of the directory Tools – where [T] is the sum of the results for all variables X_{1-9}.[4] For individual variables, X used the following gradation of weights L = 1 "low," S = 3 "strict" and M = 2 (medium) "medium." The "low" and "medium" weighting refer to a liberal approach to the pandemic control measures applied, while the "strict" weighting refers to the application of more radical measures.

The application of the given weights made it possible to establish a typology for the overall state policy towards the COVID-19 pandemic, referred to for the purposes of this chapter as the "covidian" policy. The study includes nine X-indicators, which we include in the Tools catalogue. State policy with a liberal dimension is defined by GPCI= 1–9 (since a score of 0 is considered as no action taken). Boundaries for this score were determined by adjusting for each indicator a score of 1, determining a "low" of 9 × 1. Countries with a GPCI score between 10 and 18 will be included in the group of countries with a moderate COVID-19 pandemic policy (where the boundary of the score is determined by 9 × 2 (the score for medium). A score between GPCI 19 and 27, on the other hand, will be for countries with the most restrictive policies to combat and prevent the spread of COVID-19.

It is also worth noting here that the individual actions of states may take different forms; some of them may be the most restrictive, while others may have a completely liberal dimension within the same state. It is also important to note that the subject of the study is the analysis of restrictions at the stage of tightening the policy by the state, not the stage of easing and lifting restrictions. In this case, it was important to determine what actions were taken by the EU countries at the time of developing the threat of a pandemic and whether they were of a shared or individual character.

[X₁] – other (extraordinary legal measures)

0 – no measures;
1 – introduction of a health or epidemiological emergency; and
2 – introduction of a state of emergency.

[X₂] – face covering

0 – no measures;
1 – recommendation to wear masks;
2 – partial mask wearing (only inside in public space or all situations when social distancing not possible); and
3 – requirement to wear mask in all shared/public spaces, with a fine for non-compliance.

[X₃] – remote schooling

0 – no measures;
1 – stationary teaching, recommendations for safety, and distance in schools;
2 – partial closure, hybrid teaching (only some levels or categories); and
3 – complete closure of schools and universities (online teaching).

[X₄] – remote working

0 – no measures;
1 – work with observance of sanitary conditions;
2 – recommended remote working; and

3 – requirement of closing (or working from home), except for essential workplaces (e.g. grocery stores, doctors).

[X₅] – international movement restrictions

0 – no measures;
1 – quarantine upon return from countries with high risk of disease;
2 – partial closure of borders; and
3 – border closure for entry into the country.

[X₆] – national movements restrictions and limitations of public meetings

0 – no measures;
1 – recommendations and directives for operating in public spaces; quarantine upon return from countries with high risk of disease;
2 – partial closure of borders, quarantine upon return from countries with high risk of disease; and
3 – closure of borders for entry into the country, quarantine upon return from countries at high risk of morbidity.

[X₇] – closing shops

0 – no measures;
1 – recommendation to close stores other than necessary (e.g. grocery, pharmacy);
2 – partial closure, introduction of capacity limits; and
3 – requirement of closing stores other than necessary.

[X₈] – catering and hotels

0 – no measures;
1 – catering and hotels with observance of sanitary conditions;
2 – limits on admission; and
3 – closure of catering establishments and hotels, eating out.

[X₉] – public transport restrictions

0 – no measures;
1 – observance of sanitation rules (e.g. wearing masks, social distancing);
2 – setting limits on public transport use; and
3 – negative test results or confirmation of vaccination required.

By assigning weights to the individual X-indicators, it was possible in the following section to determine which countries adopted a more liberal or radical policy of action and, above all, to make a qualitative assessment of this policy in terms of its individual or common dimension for the EU countries.

1.2   Government COVID-19 policy in EU countries

This part of the work focuses on analysing the instruments used by individual EU Member States in the fight against the COVID-19 pandemic by the governments of Austria, Belgium, Bulgaria, Croatia, Cyprus, the Czech Republic, Denmark, Estonia, Finland, France, Germany, Greece, Hungary, Ireland, Italy, Latvia, Lithuania, Luxembourg, Malta, Poland, Portugal, Romania, Slovakia, Slovenia, Spain, Sweden, and the United Kingdom. In the early days of the pandemic, member states worked to flatten the upward curve of SARS-CoV-2 cases, but in the months that followed, as they gained knowledge and experience in dealing with the threat, they developed solutions to prevent the pandemic from spreading. This may be evidenced by the so-called return to "normalcy" and the easing of a number of restrictions introduced over the summer.

The too slow introduction of restrictions in EU countries and the failure of citizens to comply with them caused a sharp incidence increase in Italy, Spain, and France (Department of Foreign Affairs of Italy, 2021; Iosa. M., Paolucci, S., & Morone G. (2020), pp. 1–2; Statistica, Cumulative number of coronavirus, 2021). Similarly, in the United Kingdom, the high number of people infected was due to a state strategy based on the pursuit of population-based immunity, adopted in the initial phase. However, given the threat posed by the exponential increase in the number of cases, new demands were made and quarantine and mandatory self-isolation were introduced (Colfer, 2020, pp. 206–208). In Belgium, on the other hand, at the onset of the pandemic, the government introduced some soft restrictive measures, including a recommendation not to hold large public events; by mid-March 2020, it was decided to impose stricter measures (Federal Public Service, Belgium. (n. d.)). Regarding the case of the Finnish "covidian" policy, it is important to note the government's quick response to the threat when the number of infections began to skyrocket in the spring of 2020. This, together with the application of extensive restrictions on public life, made the incidence of the disease slow down (Report Finland, 2020, pp. 2–3).

It is worth mentioning the case of Sweden, which in the first phase of the spread of the pandemic applied the least restrictive solutions in the EU, and no nationwide lockdown was introduced. The Swedish government's response to the COVID-19 pandemic was significantly less restrictive than that of many other EU countries, and most of its actions took the form of recommendations, unlike in other member states, where restrictions, bans, and orders were used. During the first eight months of the COVID-19 pandemic, the Swedish pandemic control strategy focused mainly on voluntary measures, with no restrictions and no total lockdown. When considering the effectiveness of the measures used and whether the Swedish case study can be taken as an example for other countries, it is worth considering that COVID-19 was not evenly spread in Sweden, given the population density. In this case, the country's capital determined COVID-19 infection rates due to its size and population density (Jonung, 2020; Karlson et al., 2020; Report Sweden, 2020, pp. 2–7).

As recommended by the WHO, during the first phase of the pandemic, EU countries decided to implement a number of measures to limit the spread of the pandemic. Although each country took an individual approach to dealing with the threat, we can distinguish a catalogue of similar solutions in the policy of EU governments, which, depending on the course of the pandemic in a given country had their national implementation. In subsequent stages, countries relied on their own experiences and the applicability of the implemented solutions. The main task for countries was to maintain social distancing, which was enforced through restrictions in the form of a ban on assembly and movement and the order to wear masks (at both the national and the international levels) together with the closure of places of public use (commercial, educational, cultural, sports, catering, and hotel facilities). Remote schooling and remote working have been used to reduce population mobility (Coronavirus pandemic in the EU, 2020).

1.2.1 Emergency legal measures – [X₁]

Stopping the development of the pandemic also required countries to introduce extraordinary legal measures. Adherence to the principle of social distancing, essential in this process, implied the limitation of certain civil liberties guaranteed by the constitution. The introduction of a state of emergency allowed the government to restrict the rights of citizens, such as freedom of movement and freedom of assembly, in order to prevent the spread of COVID-19. Therefore, some of the EU countries declared states of emergency, among others Bulgaria (Law on Measures and Actions during the State of Emergency, 2020), the Czech Republic (Czech Republic, Crisis Act, 2000; Government of the Czech Republic, 2020), Finland (Finland State of Emergency, 2020), Lithuania (The Government of the Republic of Lithuania, 2020), Latvia (Regarding Declaration of the Emergency Situation, 2020), Portugal (Decree of the President of the Republic Portugal, 2020), Romania (The Decree of the President of Romania, 2020), and Spain (Spain State of Alarm, 2020).

France had a State of Health Emergency (French Ordinance, 2020); Malta, a Public Health Emergency (Declaration of a Public Health Emergency Order, 2020); Spain, a State of Emergency (Royal Decree, 2020); Estonia, a Declaration of Emergency Situation (2020); Slovakia, a Government Resolution (2020) and Luxembourg a Grand-ducal Decree (2020); and Hungary, a State of Emergency (Hungary, Governmental Decree, 2020). In Germany, the Infectious Diseases Protection Act (Germany, the Infectious Diseases Protection Act, 2020) gave the executive branch broad powers to prevent and control infectious diseases. In Poland, the state of epidemic was introduced (Rozporządzenie Ministra Zdrowia, 2020), which gave rise to heated debates as to whether restrictions on certain civil liberties without the introduction of a state of emergency were justified.

In contrast, the Constitutions of Austria, Belgium (La Constitution Belge, 2019), and Italy (Italian Republic Constitution, 1947) have not introduced the state of emergency regulations. In the Basic Law of Austria, there were provisions on conduct in times of distress (Federal Constitutional Law of Austria, 2021); however, regulations on conduct during a pandemic are found in Consolidated Federal Law: Entire legal provision for COVID-19 (Measures Act Austria Covid Act, 2020). In Belgium, in 2020, measures were taken to adapt the constitution to pandemic conditions [Belgium, COVID-19 (I); Belgium, COVID-19 (II)]. In Italy, on January 31, 2020, the Council of Ministers' decision declared a state of emergency. In Slovenia, however, government action in a pandemic was governed by the Decree on Declaration of COVID-19 Epidemic (Odredba o razglasitvi epidemije nalezljive bolezni SARS-CoV-2, 2020), with no additional constitutional provision. The United Kingdom enacted the Coronavirus Act (2020), which introduced regulations for the operation of health services during a pandemic; no state of emergency was applied.

The Croatian government introduced a number of regulations concerning the functioning of the state in a pandemic (The Infectious Diseases Protection Act, 2020); no state of emergency was introduced there. Denmark introduced the Epidemic Act (2019), which allowed the government to impose restrictions on public gatherings, quarantine, and closure of public facilities. In response to the COVID-19 pandemic, the Dutch government did not declare a state of emergency or other extraordinary decrees. Existing legislation and regulations were considered to fully provide the instruments to address the crisis. The central legal instrument used was the COVID-19 Public Health Act of Netherlands (2020) and the Act on Security Regions (2020). The Swedish government, on the other hand, relied heavily on recommendations that were not reflected in the adoption of a state of emergency (Decisions and Guidelines of the Ministry of Health and Social Affairs, 2020). The Republic of Cyprus has followed the Quarantine Law and the Decision of Minister of Health (Quarantine Law – Decree, Chapter 260, 2020), and like the previous states did not introduce a state of emergency. Greece did not have a state of emergency, and its functioning during a pandemic was based on Acts of Legislative Content (2020). In the case of Ireland, the Ireland Health Act (2020) and the Ireland Emergency Act (2020) were introduced.

Thus, in the case of extraordinary remedies, we do not find a uniform approach; the states to their own extent have made regulations with respect to legal resources and the laws binding in the state.

1.2.2   Face covering – [X₂]

1.2.2   Face covering – [X$_2$]

A number of hygiene recommendations (e.g. frequent hand washing and disinfection) have been introduced in the Community Member States, and in most countries, the obligation to wear masks in public spaces has been reduced (e.g. in Austria, Belgium, Cyprus, Croatia, the Czech Republic, Denmark, Ireland, Estonia, France, Germany, Greece, Italy, Latvia, Luxembourg, the Netherlands, Malta, Portugal, Romania, Slovakia, and the United Kingdom) (The Response Measures Database, n.d.). In other countries, the wearing of masks was mandatory at the start of the pandemic both indoors and outdoors (e.g. Bulgaria, Poland, Slovenia, Spain, Hungary), while the United Kingdom (Government UK, n.d.) issued an order to wear masks only on public transport, and in Denmark – only at the airports (see Table 1.1). Belgium imposed a nearly universal obligation to wear masks in public spaces and social contact (without a mask) was restricted. Violation of the regulation in Belgium was punishable by a fine. In summer, the obligation to cover the nose and mouth was reduced to public places only and when social distancing was impossible, the wearing of a mask was obligatory (Belgian Federal Public Service, n.d.). In Austria, in places with 3-G rules (vaccinated, tested, and recovered), the wearing of masks was not obligatory (Austrian Federal Ministry for Social Affairs, n.d.). In Portugal (Alto Comissariado para as Migrações, 2021), Slovakia (IOM Migration Information Centre, 2021), Hungary (Hungary, Governmental Decision, 2020), and Greece (Covid-19 in Greece, 2020), covering the nose and mouth was mandatory when using public transport as well as in public places. Fines were imposed for non-compliance (Portugal between Euro 120 and 350, Greece 150, Slovakia over 1000). During the first wave of the epidemic, masks were also mandatory in all enclosed public spaces and means of transport in Italy (Department of Foreign Affairs of Italy, 2021), and France (Governement de France, n.d.), then only in public spaces. Similarly, in Bulgaria, Croatia, and Romania, failure to comply with the obligation to wear masks in public spaces was punishable by a fine (Bulgaria travel advice, n.d.; Croatia introduces new measures, 2020; Ministry of Health. Romania, n.d.). The most liberal approach was taken by the governments of Sweden (Report Sweden, 2020), by recommending the wearing of masks in public spaces, and Latvia – by recommending keeping a distance (Government of Latvia, n.d.).

In Spain and Malta, the obligation to wear masks has been reduced to closed and open public spaces (where a distance of one and a half metres was not possible), with a fine of about 100 euros (Legislation Mandatory Use of Medical or Cloth Masks, 2020). In Austria, Cyprus, the Netherlands, Ireland, Germany, Latvia, Luxembourg, and Slovenia, it was mandatory to wear a mask only in public spaces (e.g. public transport) and in situations where it was not possible to keep a social distance (Cyprus, 2020; Government of the Netherlands, n.d.; The Governing Mayor of Berlin, 2021; Government of Ireland, n.d.; Luxembourg. COVID-19 information, n.d.). Austria has made the wearing of FFP2 masks mandatory. Estonia has imposed nose and mouth covering in stores and places of public use (Estonian Government, n.d.). The Czech authorities mandated the wearing of FFP2 masks, not allowing the use of surgical masks. The order applied to places of public use, with a penalty of about 10,000 Czech koruna for non-compliance (Government of the Czech Republic, 2020.). In Denmark, at the beginning of the pandemic, the obligation to cover the nose and mouth in public transport was introduced; in 2021, the obligation to wear masks in public spaces (except airports) was abolished; it is recommended to wear a mask when visiting a hospital (Danish Ministry of Health, n.d.). In Poland, in the first phase, the wearing of masks was obligatory only in public spaces, whereas at the beginning of the second wave of the pandemic the wearing of masks was obligatory in every place even outdoors. Moreover, in case of lack of a mask, a fine was imposed (Website of the Republic of Poland, n.d.).

Lithuania, Finland (Report Finland, 2020), and Sweden were among the few European countries that did not require masks. In Lithuania, the use of them was recommended, although not universally required as in other countries, and a distance of at least one metre was required in public spaces (The Official Development Agency of the City of Vilnius, 2021; Lithuania). In Sweden and Finland, the regulations on nose and mouth covering were recommended for closed public spaces such as public transport, stores, and schools. It is interesting to note that despite the introduction in other EU countries and the WHO of the recommendation to wear face masks in public spaces, the Karolinska Institutet in Stockholm (2020) suggested face covering only in places where physical distance was considered impossible. Of all EU countries, Sweden, Latvia, and Finland took the most liberal approach to the obligation of mask wearing, as covering the nose and mouth was

Table 1.1 Face covering in EU countries

Country	Injunction/recommendation/fine	
1 Austria	Requirement to wear FFP2 masks in public spaces.	2
2 Belgium	Requirement to wear masks in public spaces. Lack of mask punishable by fine.	3
3 Bulgaria	Requirement to wear masks in public spaces. Lack of mask punishable by fine.	3
4 Croatia	Requirement to wear masks in public spaces. Lack of mask punishable by fine.	3
5 Republic of Cyprus	Requirement to wear masks in public spaces.	2
6 Czech Republic	Requirement to wear FFP2 masks in public spaces. Lack of mask punishable by fine.	3
7 Denmark	Requirement to wear masks at airports.	1
8 Estonia	Requirement to cover nose and mouth in shops and public places.	2
9 Finland	No requirement to wear masks. Recommended when social distancing impossible.	1
10 France	Masks required on public transport and in closed public spaces.	2
11 Germany	Masks required on public transport and in public spaces.	2
12 Greece	Covering nose and mouth required when using public transport and in public spaces. Lack of mask punishable by fine.	3
13 Hungary	Requirement to wear a mask when using public transport and in public spaces. Lack of mask punishable by fine.	3
14 Ireland	Masks required in closed public spaces where social distancing impossible.	2
15 Italy	Masks required in all closed public spaces and on public transport. Lack of mask punishable by fine.	3
16 Latvia	Requirement of mask wearing only in public spaces.	2
17 Lithuania	No requirement of mask wearing; social distancing is necessary.	1
18 Luxembourg	Masks required only in public spaces where social distancing is impossible.	2
19 Malta	Requirement to wear masks in public spaces. Lack of mask punishable by fine.	3
20 Netherlands	Masks required only in public spaces.	2
21 Poland	Requirement to wear masks in public spaces. Initially also outdoors. Lack of mask punishable by fine.	3
22 Portugal	Covering of nose and mouth required on public transport and in public spaces. Lack of mask punishable by fine.	3
23 Romania	Requirement to wear masks in public spaces. Lack of mask punishable by fine.	3
24 Slovakia	Nose and mouth covering required on public transport and in public spaces. Lack of mask punishable by fine.	3
25 Slovenia	Requirement to wear masks only in public spaces.	2
26 Spain	Requirement of wearing masks limited to closed and open public spaces. Lack of mask punishable by fine.	3
27 Sweden	No requirement of mask wearing.	1
28 United Kingdom	Masks required on public transport.	2

Source: Own elaboration.

the recommendation when social distance was not possible. The rest of the countries introduced the obligation to wear masks in closed and open public spaces; in addition, some countries introduced fines for not respecting the order (e.g. Belgium, Bulgaria, Croatia, the Czech Republic, Greece, Poland, Portugal, Romania, Spain). (Coronavirus pandemic in the EU, 2020).

1.2.3   Remote schooling – [X_3] and remote working – [X_4]

The transition to distance learning has been a major challenge for many countries, particularly in the context of the technical preparation of schools and providers of this process and also the skills of both teachers and students to adapt to the new reality. Working remotely with techni-cal solutions, on the other hand, was a recommended measure, especially against the background of distance learning, and for many parents, it was even a desirable solution. Not in all sectors of the economy, this solution was possible.

In Italy, as the first country, at the beginning of the pandemic, when the country recorded a significant increase in disease and mortality, radical restrictions were introduced, including the complete closure of all educa-tional institutions and restrictions on the mobility of the population (only commuting to work) and a significant emphasis on remote working (indus-tries that could not provide online services were closed) (Ministry of Health. Italy, n.d.). In Austria, Denmark, Lithuania, and Latvia, remote schooling was introduced at the beginning of the pandemic and lasted until the end of 2020, and at the beginning of 2021, universities began to open, giving institutions the right to make their own decisions in relation to the teaching/ learning process during the pandemic. In the sphere of work, recommenda-tions for remote working in all possible industries were put forward. Service providers with close contact to customers (hairdressers and massage thera-pists) were required to have a negative PCR test (Federal Ministry of Health Republic of Austria, n.d.; Danish Ministry of Health, n.d.; The Ministry of Health. Lithuania, 2021; The Ministry of Health. Latvia, 2021). In Belgium, primary and secondary schools were closed in the first and second waves; this was not repeated in the next wave. The Belgian government used the recommendation of online working, but it was soon made compulsory (World Bank, 2020; Federal Public Services, Belgium, n.d.). In Bulgaria and Greece, on the other hand, a solution for remote working was intro-duced for only 50% of employees, and remote schooling was introduced (Bulgaria. Health System Response Monitor, 2021; Greece. National Public Health Organization, 2021). In Croatia, on the other hand, remote teaching/ learning has been introduced, as well as recommendations to work remotely, provided it was possible, and some limitations imposed in the physical contact of employees through different shifts and social distance (Government of the Republic of Croatia, 2020; Coronavirus in Croatia, 2021). In Cyprus, remote schooling was introduced at the beginning of the pandemic; in the later stages, sanitary standards were observed in the teaching process together with limitation of the number of people in the teaching room and the need for testing, vaccination, or recovery certificate for teachers. Teleworking was introduced in the private sector and the necessity of observing distance in the public sector (Ministry of Health Cyprus, n.d.). At the beginning of the pandemic, remote teaching/learning was made compulsory also in the Czech Republic; at a later stage, onsite schooling was reintroduced with the observance of hygiene rules and social distancing. For work, the recommendation was to use remote working, where possible, together with the requirement for the employers to test their employees (Ministry of Health of Czech Republic, n.d.).

In France, Germany, Ireland, Estonia, Malta, the Netherlands, Portugal, Romania, Slovakia, Spain, and Slovenia, distance schooling was in force during the development phase of the pandemic. Additional protective measures, i.e. the testing of teachers and students and the obligation to wear masks, were also applied after the return to onsite teaching/learning. In the case of work, recommendations for remote working were applied whenever the profile allowed it (Governement de France, n.d.; Federal Ministry of Health. Germany, n.d.; Government of Ireland, n.d.; Estonian Government, n.d.; Ministry of Health. Malta, n.d.; Ministry of Health, Welfare and Sport. Netherlands, 2021; Ministry of Health, Consumer Affairs and Social Welfare. Spain, n.d.; Ministry of Health. Portugal, n.d.; Ministry of Public Health. Romania, n.d.; Ministry of Health. Slovakia, n.d.; Ministry of Health. Slovenia, n.d.).

Already in the early phase of the pandemic, educational institutions were closed in Finland and Luxembourg. However, despite the state of emergency in Finland, remote teaching/learning in upper primary and secondary schools ended quickly, and students returned to classes in a hybrid system that alternated between school and home learning. The transition of schools to e-learning was facilitated by the fact that Finnish schools were equipped with computers and that students used them on a daily basis (Ministry of Social Affairs and Health Finland, n.d.). Educational institutions in Luxembourg have also transitioned to hybrid teaching. Remote working has been recommended for all possible industries (Ministry of Health. Luxembourg, n.d.).

In Sweden, public spaces, kindergartens, and schools for children up to the age of 16 were operational throughout the pandemic, and schools for older children were closed for only three months. In Sweden, an important recommendation was to work from home if possible and to minimise leaving home. The recommendations were voluntary, however, resulting in Swedes adhering to these recommendations (Public Health Agency of Sweden, n.d.).

In Poland and Hungary, state authorities had already introduced distance learning for all levels of schools and universities at the beginning of the pandemic. In the case of universities, the return to school did not take place until autumn of 2021, with schools having online or onsite classes depending on the upward or downward trend in the pandemic (Hungary, Governmental Decision no. 1102/2020, 2020; Hungary, Health System Response Monitor, 2021; Ministry of Health Poland, n.d.). In the case of work, many sectors of the economy have moved to remote working where possible and industries where it was not possible to e-work or maintain social distancing have been closed (catering, leisure, services, etc.). For the United Kingdom, it was very important to maintain continuity in the education process; in the early stages of the pandemic, government policy was somewhat more liberal (in relation to other countries). The United Kingdom was the last to introduce distance teaching/learning. As a result of the decrease in the number of cases of the disease, onsite schooling was resumed with the requirement of maintaining sanitary standards and social distance. In the case of work, government recommendations were reduced to remote working and social distancing (UK Government Department for Education, 2020; UK Government, n.d.).

To sum up the theme, it is worth mentioning that the policies of member states regarding remote working and teaching/learning were significantly similar and consistent. In their actions, most state governments recommended limiting employee mobility through remote working (when possible) and limiting employee contact when working onsite. In the case of teaching/learning, most countries introduced remote schooling at all levels of education. The rise and fall of morbidity determined the next steps of government actions, from a return to onsite schooling, hybrid teaching/learning, and/or the introduction of remote schooling. In this context, most countries acted in a similar way, except in the case of Sweden, where the government policy had a significantly different dimension, with liberal recommendations rather than restrictions (see Table 1.2).

1.2.4   *International movement restrictions – [X_5]*

Despite solutions at the national level imposed by individual countries, EU-wide measures have also been introduced. Thus, in March 2020, a decision was made to restrict non-essential travel to the EU by those who do not hold citizenship of EU countries, the EEA, Switzerland, the United Kingdom, and other special cases. Schengen countries agreed to close the external borders of the European Union to non-Community nationals for a period of

Table 1.2 Schooling and working remotely in EU countries

Country	Online classes (+) onsite classes (−) hybrid classes (+/−)	Results	Work from home (+) onsite (−) recommendations for online work (+/−)	Results
	Schooling		*Work*	
1 **Austria**	+	3	+/−	2
2 **Belgium**	+	3	+	3
3 **Bulgaria**	+	3	+/−	2
4 **Croatia**	+	3	+/−	2
5 **Cyprus**	+	3	+	3
6 **Czech Republic**	+	3	+/−	2
7 **Denmark**	+	3	+/−	2
8 **Estonia**	+	3	+/−	2
9 **Finland**	+/−	2	+/−	2
10 **France**	+	3	+/−	2
11 **Germany**	+	3	+/−	2
12 **Greece**	+	3	+/−	2
13 **Hungary**	+	3	+/−	2
14 **Ireland**	+	3	+/−	2
15 **Italy**	+	3	+/−	2
16 **Latvia**	+	3	+/−	2
17 **Lithuania**	+	3	+/−	2
18 **Luxembourg**	+/−	2	+/−	2
19 **Malta**	+	3	+/−	2
20 **Netherlands**	+	3	+/−	2
21 **Poland**	+	3	+/−	2
22 **Portugal**	+	3	+/−	2
23 **Romania**	+	3	+/−	2
24 **Slovakia**	+	3	+/−	2
25 **Slovenia**	+	3	+/−	2
26 **Spain**	+	3	+/−	2
27 **Sweden**	−	1	−	1
28 **United Kingdom**	+	3	+/−	2

Source: Own elaboration.

30 days (European Commission, 2020, March 16). This occurred despite the fact that, under EU law, the European Commission did not have the power to rule how restrictions would be enforced in member states. However, there was an exchange of information within the EU regarding the effectiveness of the actions applied by separate states, and it was recommended in this case to unify and coordinate actions towards the external states of the EU.

Most European countries decided to close their borders and/or introduce a number of restrictions against crossing them. In addition, quarantine and/ or testing was imposed for those who without vaccination. The decision to completely close borders was made by Belgium, Croatia, Cyprus, the Czech Republic, Denmark, Estonia, Finland, Hungary, Latvia, Lithuania, Malta, Poland, Slovenia, and Spain. Partial restrictions (entry ban for citizens of certain countries) has been introduced by Austria (bordering with Germany, Switzerland, Liechtenstein, the Czech Republic, Slovakia, and Hungary were closed until June 2020), Bulgaria (restricting entry for citizens of Italy, Spain, France, Germany, and the Netherlands), and Greece (closing borders with Albania and North Macedonia); open borders only for EU citizens were made available by the Netherlands, Luxembourg, Romania, and Sweden. Additionally, Austria banned all arrivals from Italy, China's Hubei Province, Iran, and South Korea, except for travellers with negative test results. In June 2020, travel restrictions were lifted in most European countries (Bayer & Cokeleare, 2020; Hantrais & Letablier, 2021).

In addition, solutions were adopted related to the need for negative tests and/or quarantine and, in subsequent stages, confirmation of vaccination against COVID-19. In Austria, Belgium, Bulgaria, the Czech Republic, Denmark, Estonia, France. Germany, Greece, Hungary, Ireland, Italy, Latvia, Lithuania, Malta, the Netherlands, Poland, Portugal, Romania, Slovenia, Slovakia, Spain, and the United Kingdom, testing and quarantine were introduced for returnees from high-risk or "red zone"[5] countries, where incidence rate was much higher than that in other countries (Hirsch, 2020; The Response Measures Database, n.d.; Lithuania, Department of Foreign Affairs, 2021). In the next phase, after the introduction of the COVID-19 vaccine, vaccinated persons entering the country were exempt from quarantine. In Sweden, on the other hand, the Public Health Agency recommended that people returning from high-risk countries should avoid contact with people and stay at home, and get tested (Jonung, 2020; Public Health Agency of Sweden, n.d.). Croatia allowed entry for citizens from the "green zone" countries; citizens from other countries had to present a PCR test result (Government of the Republic of Croatia, 2020). Entry to Cyprus was also permitted upon presentation of a negative test result or confirmation of vaccination (Ministry of Health Cyprus, n.d.). In Finland, restrictions were placed on travel to non-European countries, and those entering the country from European Union territories had to undergo quarantine and testing. Border control was also in place at all times, and entry into Finland was not possible without a valid reason (Ministry of Social Affairs and Health, Finland, n.d.).

The reduction in the incidence numbers during the summer allowed countries to loosen restrictions, primarily to allow the entry of foreign nationals.

This was particularly important for countries where tourism is one of the relevant economic areas (e.g. Greece, Italy, Spain, Croatia). These countries allowed tourists to enter the country on presentation of a negative test result and/or confirmation of full vaccination.

1.2.5 *National movements restriction and public meetings – [X₆]*

Closing external borders was a measure to limit population mobility and thus the spread of the virus. However, some countries have also taken measures to close or restrict population movements within the internal structure of the country. Internal bans related to limiting participation in public events were introduced, by closing or imposing limits on sports or cultural facilities (theatres, museums, cinemas, etc.). Most EU countries were introducing national lockdowns in March 2020 (the exceptions were Italy, which did so on January 31, 2020; Lithuania on February 26 and Sweden on April 4). Linda Hantrais and Marie-Thérèse Letablier (2021) summarised the introduction of national lockdowns in EU countries after the first three COVID-19-related deaths. Sixteen countries were found to have introduced lockdowns before the third death was reported in the country. Slovenia took action long before the fatalities were recorded (42 days), Malta (30), Lithuania (28), Slovakia (26), Italy (25), and Latvia (30). Austria, Estonia, the Czech Republic, Croatia, Cyprus, Finland, Luxembourg, Romania, Poland, and Portugal also declared a state of emergency a few days/several days before the third COVID-19 death was reported, while Bulgaria, Denmark, Greece, Hungary, the Netherlands, and Spain made a declaration within days after the third death. Belgium (15), France (13), Germany (13), Ireland (12), Sweden (19), and the United Kingdom (14) declared a lockdown more than ten days after the third death in the country (Hantrais & Letablier, 2021, pp. 42–44).

The pandemic started to spread in Austria from March 2020, already at the very beginning actions were taken about the introduction of the first lockdown; all outdoor meetings above 500 people and indoors above 100 people were cancelled. In the next step, leaving the house was permitted only due to necessary outings (e.g. shopping, work, physical activity). Places of public use (cinemas, theatres, museums) were closed (Federal Ministry of Health Republic of Austria, n.d.). In Belgium, the Czech Republic, Estonia, and Greece social distancing measures were tightened, including bans on all outdoor gatherings, including sports and cultural events (The Response Measures Database, n.d.). In Belgium, walking, running, and cycling were allowed within limits of observing social distance; the need to remain physically active was seen as a key measure for maintaining the mental and physical health of the population. Outside of households, people could only meet in groups of up to four people while respecting the rules of physical distance. In the severely affected province of Antwerp, a curfew was imposed to avoid gatherings of larger groups of (mostly young) people, mainly in food-serving establishments (Luyten & Schokkaert, 2021; Belgian Federal Public Service, n.a). In Bulgaria, as well as in Croatia, Cyprus, the Czech Republic, Lithuania, the Netherlands, Slovakia, and Slovenia, attendance limits were set for public and private gatherings, and occupancy limits were introduced for places of entertainment while keeping a distance and using face masks. Additional restrictions in these countries were applied to restrict the operation of fitness clubs, requiring them to maintain adequate space in square metres per person, to disinfect equipment, and to ventilate the premises. Person limits were also applied to places providing entertainment. Recommendations were made for people over 60 and people with medical conditions to avoid crowded public places. In Ireland, six-week strict movement restrictions were initially applied only within the residential area (The Response Measures Database, n.d.; Government of Ireland, n.d.; Ministry of Health, Welfare and Sport, Netherlands, 2021).

In Finland, the first action of the authorities was to impose a lockdown for about two months. It was forbidden to move around the country. Finnish measures to combat COVID-19 were mainly based on recommendations related to the use of social distancing. Respecting these recommendations for the citizens was not particularly difficult, considering the low population density in the country. A positive factor of the government's actions is that they have not led to a complete shutdown of the Finnish economy, nor have they introduced a curfew. In Finland, a significant increase in cases in March 2021 and the threat posed by a new strain of the virus (commonly known as British) forced the Finnish government to impose a state of emergency (Report Finland, 2020; Ministry of Social Affairs and Health, Finland, 2020; Finland, n.d.). In Denmark, Estonia, and France, significant limits were imposed on public spaces (cinemas, museums, and theatres) and the organisation of public meetings. The use of masks in enclosed public spaces and appropriate distance has been mandated (Danish Ministry of Health, n.d.; Governement de France, n.d.; Estonian Government, n.d.). Sweden did not implement quarantine for infected persons in households. Social distance was one recommendation, not a restriction as it was only mandatory in public places such as restaurants and when visiting elderly care homes (Karlson et al., 2020).

Italy was the first country to implement a partial lockdown, closing the Lombardy region and towns in the province of Lodi as a result of the exponential increase in incidence in that part of Italy. Another action by the Italian government was to impose a state-wide quarantine and a complete restriction on the movement of the population (Ministry of Health Italy, n.d.). Very strict measures were introduced in Italy and Spain due to the significant increase in the incidence of the disease: a ban on public gatherings, family visits, and social gatherings, which were to enforce respecting the obligation to stay at home. It was only possible to go out for work or shopping, if necessary (Ministry of Health, Consumer Affairs and Social Welfare, Spain, n.d.). In Germany, on the other hand, no restrictive measures were introduced in the context of freedom of movement; going to the store, travelling to work or physical activities were allowed. The government action was to limit the mobility of the population rather than to prohibit it (Federal Ministry of Health, Germany, n.d.).

In Poland, at the beginning of the pandemic, a number of prohibitions were introduced to limit the mobility of the population (obligation to leave home only when necessary, order to limit social gatherings). Places of public use (sports centres, cinemas, museums, and theatres) and the organisation of all kinds of mass events were shut down. Moreover, it was also forbidden to visit forests at a certain time. An unusual solution was also the closure of cemeteries in 2020 before All Souls Day, in order to avoid gatherings at cemeteries, and a ban on going out on New Year's Eve without a serious reason (Website of the Republic of Poland, n.d.; Ministry of Health Poland, n.d.). In Portugal, a negative test or confirmation of vaccination was required to use public places (cinemas, restaurants, and hotels) (Ministry of Health Portugal, n.d.). In Hungary, the government banned events and meetings with a limit of more than 100 people inside or more than 500 people outside. In a further step, all public events of a sporting cultural, scientific nature, protests, assemblies, or any form of public gatherings inside or outside were banned (Hungary, Health System Response Monitor, 2021). Ireland, Latvia, Luxembourg, Malta, and Romania have applied similar measures to sports and recreation venues. Significant restrictions and limits on the number of persons have been applied in public spaces, along with orders to wear masks and keep a distance (The Response Measures Database, n.d.; Luxembourg, COVID-19 information, n.d.; Ministry of Health, Romania, n.d.). In the United Kingdom, restrictions on public gatherings and the closure of cinemas, theatres, museums, gyms, and swimming pools have been enforced to ensure social distance (UK, Department of Health and Social Care, n.d.).

Analysing the actions of the countries in the context of national movement restrictions, it is worth noting that in this case the actions of the countries can be divided into complete closure of public space (cinemas, museums, theatres, exhibitions, gyms, etc.) and its partial closure (by introducing limits on the number of people present). The only exception in this case was Sweden, which used the given restrictions as recommendations in maintaining social distance, not leading to the closure of public space (see Table 1.3).

Table 1.3 National and international movement restrictions

	Country	International	National
1	Austria	3	3
2	Belgium	3	3
3	Bulgaria	3	2
4	Croatia	3	2
5	Cyprus	3	2
6	Czech Republic	3	2
7	Denmark	3	2
8	Estonia	3	2
9	Finland	3	2
10	France	3	2
11	Germany	3	2
12	Greece	3	3
13	Hungary	3	3
14	Ireland	3	3
15	Italy	3	3
16	Latvia	3	3
17	Lithuania	3	2
18	Luxembourg	2	3
19	Malta	3	3
20	Netherlands	2	2
21	Poland	3	3
22	Portugal	3	3
23	Romania	2	3
24	Slovakia	3	2
25	Slovenia	3	2
26	Spain	3	3
27	Sweden	2	1
28	United Kingdom	3	3

Source: Own elaboration.

1.2.6   *Shop closing – [X₇]*

Restrictions imposed on the operation of stores were one of the key solutions proposed by EU governments. It mainly amounted to closing non-essential shops and introducing a limit in the number of people present in stores belonging to the most essential categories (i.e. grocery stores, drug stores, pharmacies). In Austria, Cyprus, Estonia, Spain, Denmark, Hungary, Ireland, Italy, Latvia, Lithuania, Luxembourg, Malta, the Netherlands, Romania, Slovakia, Slovenia, and the United Kingdom, all stores were closed in the initial phase, except for essential stores and shopping malls. Covering the nose and mouth with masks in stores was mandatory. As a result of the reduction in the number of cases in the country, other stores and large areas were gradually opened (The Response Measures Database, n.d.). In Belgium, construction supply and garden centres and stores that did not stock necessities (such as groceries, cosmetics and chemicals, and medicines) were closed as early as March 2020 as a result of the lockdown. In addition, limits were placed on the number of people who could be in the stores at one time, along with the obligation to disinfect hands and wear a mask. Sales at markets were prohibited. In addition, no alcohol could be purchased after 8 p.m. In the second wave of the pandemic, the government almost immediately reinstated the stringent measures used in the first wave with minimal relaxation; just as in the first phase, only stores supplying essential products were allowed to operate (Luyten & Schokkaert, 2021; World Bank., 2020).

Similarly, in Bulgaria, Croatia, the Czech Republic, France, Greece, and Poland, all but non-essential stores were closed during the early stages of the pandemic. In particular, restrictions applied to large area stores (e.g. construction supplies) and shopping malls. In case of stores supplying basic needs, people limits, the obligation to keep a distance, and to cover one's nose and mouth were introduced. In addition, in Poland, shopping hours for seniors (10–12) were introduced, when only authorised persons over 60 years of age could do shopping, in order to ensure that older people could avoid crowded public places (The Response Measures Database, n.d.; Ministry of Health Poland. (n.d.)). In Finland, Germany, and Portugal, stores operated under a strict sanitary regime setting a limit on the number of people in the store (Federal Ministry of Health, Germany, n.d.; Ministry of Social Affairs and Health, Finland, 2021; Portugal, Covid-19 information (2021)). In the case of Portugal, additional restrictions were placed on store hours during the week, weekends, and holidays, reducing hours of operation. In Sweden, on the other hand, no restrictions were placed on the closing of non-essential stores, and all stores (including construction supplies and malls) operated normally during the pandemic. In addition, there was no requirement to wear a mask in stores. Covering one's nose and mouth and keeping one's distance were recommended, not mandated (Report Sweden, 2020).

To sum up the theme, it should be acknowledged that the majority of European Union countries have applied the solution of closing large stores (including construction supplies and shopping malls) apart from the so-called essential retail stores, in order to reduce the mobility of the population. This forced people to go out only for essential purchases in grocery stores and pharmacies. In the case of Germany, Portugal, and Finland, such stores were not closed completely, but restrictions on the number of people and sanitary standards were introduced. The most liberal approach was taken by Sweden which did not close stores but only recommended covering the nose and mouth and keeping a social distance.

1.2.7   Catering and hotels – [X₈]

1.2.7   Catering and hotels – [X_8]

Catering and hotel establishments were included in the catalogue of entities to which restrictions were applied due to high risk of disease and limited possibilities of keeping social distance in such places. Some of the countries have introduced limits on the number of people staying in given places, and in the more restrictive cases, the places have been ordered to close, with the possibility (in case of gastronomic facilities) of selling take-away meals.

In Austria, a number of measures have been introduced to prevent the spread of the virus in catering establishments. In the early stages of the pandemic, these establishments were closed, and service provision was limited to the sale of takeaway meals (Austrian Federal Ministry for Social Affairs, n.d.). In Austria and Germany, 3-G rules were introduced, a certificate, negative test, or confirmation of COVID-19 infection was required for people visiting catering establishments, masks had to be worn indoors and distances had to be kept. It should be mentioned that in Germany, regulations in relation to catering were introduced by individual Länder, depending on the incidence rate, but these were not nationwide restrictions (Federal Ministry of Health, Germany, n.d.). In Bulgaria, limits of 50% occupancy were applied for restaurants and restrictions were placed on the opening hours of establishments, while bars and discotheques were completely closed. In addition, it was mandatory to wear masks and observe social distance. Full capacity for gastronomy was only possible for vaccinated persons or those with a negative test result (Bulgaria, Health System Response Monitor, 2021). In Belgium, there was a complete closure of catering establishments, and later a result of loosening restrictions, establishments were open, although customers in pubs and restaurants had to register to help define possible locations of infection (Federal Public Service, Belgium (n. d.)).

In the Czech Republic, Croatia, Greece, Ireland, and Portugal, in both the first and second waves of the pandemic, bars, restaurants, and other catering and hotel establishments were closed (Government of the Czech Republic, 2020; Covid-19 in Greece, 2020; Colfer, 2020; Coronavirus in Croatia, 2021). As a result of the reduction in the number of cases, restrictions were eased in all EU countries and catering and hotel establishments were reopened. After the opening of restaurants, the government in Croatia introduced restrictions on the operation of establishments and a ban on the sale of alcohol after 10 p.m. In Cyprus, occupancy limits were introduced and people with a negative PCR test and who had been vaccinated were allowed to use indoor establishments (Ministry of Health Cyprus, n.d.). Croatia, on the other hand, additionally, banned the sale of alcohol between 10 p.m. and 6 a.m. And in Finland and Denmark, fast-food outlets were closed as a result of the government's quick response. After the easing of restrictions, service establishments reopened, although various restrictions remained in place – for example, restaurants and hotels limited the number of available tables (Ministry of Social Affairs and Health, Finland, 2021; Danish Health Authority (n.d.)). In France, Greece, Latvia, Lithuania, Luxembourg, Malta, the Netherlands, Romania, and Slovenia, catering and hotel establishments were completely closed; the use of restaurant meals was only possible for take away. After opening, the use of restaurants was possible with a limited occupancy and observance of the sanitary rules. In France, a health passport was required (The Response Measures Database, n.d.).

In Ireland, Estonia, and Hungary, following the previous closure of establishments to takeaways only, they were allowed to open on the condition that the persons using them had a certificate, a negative test result, or a COVID-19 certificate; persons without these documents could only use the services of the establishment for takeaways (Estonian Government, n.d.; Hungary, Health System Response Monitor, 2021; Government of Ireland, n.d.).

In Italy, following an exponential rise in the incidence of the disease, restrictive measures have been taken, including a complete ban on going out of the house, so that catering services were only available for takeaways (Ministry of Health Italy, n.d.). Catering and hotels in Poland were closed; in the case of catering, it was possible to sell take-away meals, while hotels were initially open to business travellers (later the establishments were completely closed), with occupancy limits set for hotels. In subsequent stages, as a result of loosening restrictions, first limits were introduced for these places, and then, all restrictions were eventually lifted (Website of the Republic of Poland, n.d.). In Spain and the United Kingdom, catering (takeaways only) and hotel establishments were initially closed, and in subsequent phases, as the incidence of the disease decreased, establishments were gradually opened and occupancy limits introduced (Government UK, n.d.; Ministry of Health, Consumer Affairs and Social Welfare, Spain, n.d.). In Slovakia, it was mandatory to use catering only in outside conditions with the requirement of a negative test result (Ministry of Health. Slovakia, n.d.). In Sweden, on the other hand, the most liberal approach to catering was followed with bars, restaurants, and hotels operating throughout the pandemic. The government made a number of recommendations for citizens using these establishments, including keeping a distance, occupancy limits, sanitation rules, and covering the nose and mouth in public places (Report Sweden, 2020).

In summary, the complete closure of catering and hospitality establishments was a common practice in many countries at the initial stage of the pandemic, in which case, take-away services were allowed. As a result of the reduction in the number of cases of disease, restrictions were gradually eased, including the opening of establishments subject to certain rules and restrictions (occupancy limits, sanitary standards, etc.). An exception in this case was Sweden, which recommended restrictions related to catering, e.g. maintaining the distance and the occupancy limits, without introducing significant formal restrictions (see Table 1.4).

Table 1.4 Restrictions on stores, catering and hotels, and transport

	Country	Restrictions		
		Shops	*Restaurants and hotels*	*Transport*
1	Austria	3	3	2
2	Belgium	3	3	2
3	Bulgaria	3	3	2
4	Croatia	3	3	2
5	Republic of Cyprus	3	3	3
6	Czech Republic	3	3	2
7	Denmark	3	3	2
8	Estonia	3	3	2
9	Finland	2	3	2
10	France	3	3	2
11	Germany	2	3	2
12	Greece	3	3	2
13	Hungary	3	3	2
14	Ireland	3	3	2
15	Italy	3	3	2
16	Latvia	3	3	2
17	Lithuania	3	3	2
18	Luxembourg	3	3	2
19	Malta	3	3	2
20	Netherlands	3	3	2
21	Poland	3	3	2
22	Portugal	2	3	2
23	Romania	3	3	2
24	Slovakia	3	3	2
25	Slovenia	3	3	2
26	Spain	3	3	2
27	Sweden	1	1	1
28	United Kingdom	3	3	2

Source: Own elaboration.

1.2.8   *Public transport restriction – [X₉]*

Public transport is an important part of the state infrastructure; therefore, it was not possible to completely restrict or close this industry; in EU countries, restrictions were introduced to ensure social distance. In all EU countries (except Sweden and Denmark), nose and mouth covering on public transport and maintaining social distance have been made mandatory (Karolinska Institutet in Stockholm, 2020; Danish Ministry of Health, n.d.). In Sweden, this was considered a recommendation, whereas in Denmark, this obligation was only imposed at the airport. The Danish government has allowed the use of public air transport provided that there was a one-metre gap between passengers. In Croatia (Croatia introduces new measures, 2020; Coronavirus in Croatia, 2021) and the Czech Republic (Government of the Czech Republic, 2020.), limits have been introduced for public transport (buses, trains, and public transport) so that a given mode of transport could only have 40% of transport capacity occupied, in Italy 50%, Spain50%, Greece 65%, and Slovakia 1/3 of the capacity. In Cyprus, a negative test or confirmation of vaccination and the obligation to cover the mouth and nose were required in order to use transport (Cyprus, 2020). In France, long-distance public transport required health passports (Governement de France (n.d.)). The Polish government in turn introduced limits for people on public transport of 50% of the seating limit or 30% of the seating and standing limit. Due to a reduction in the number of diseases, the limits on public transport have been abolished, although the obligation to cover the nose and mouth is still in force (Ministry of Health Poland, n.d.). It is also worth noting that as a result of international movement restrictions related to the closure of borders, the EU countries have also introduced measures related to the suspension of international flights.

The results obtained for individual restrictions in the EU countries made it possible to determine a separate Governments Policy COVID Index [GPCI] score for each country. This, in turn, made it possible to classify them into a specific type according to the established typology and group the countries according to the adopted index "low," "medium," and "strict." The overall GPCI score for each country (Table 1.5) allows us to conclude that all countries except Sweden fall within the typology into the group of countries that have applied restrictive "covidian" policies to a large extent, GPCI score = 19 –27 points. In the case of Sweden, GPCI score = 9 points indicates that the policy was largely liberal in nature (see Table 1.5).

$[X_1]$ – legal measures
$[X_2]$ – masks
$[X_3]$ – remote schooling
$[X_4]$ – remote work
$[X_5]$ – international movement restrictions
$[X_6]$ – national movement restrictions and public meetings limitations
$[X_7]$ – shop closing
$[X_8]$ – catering and hotels
$[X_9]$ – public transport restrictions

It is worth noting that the 27 countries that fall into the restrictive group have varying GPCI scores from 19 to 25 points. None of the states scored

Table 1.5 EU COVID-19 restriction scores

	Country	X_1	X_2	X_3	X_4	X_5	X_6	X_7	X_8	X_9	GPCI results
1	Austria	1	2	3	2	3	3	3	3	2	22
2	Belgium	0	3	3	3	3	3	3	3	3	24
3	Bulgaria	2	3	3	2	3	2	3	3	2	23
4	Croatia	0	3	3	2	3	2	3	3	2	21
5	Republic of Cyprus	0	2	3	3	3	2	3	3	3	22
6	Czech Republic	2	3	3	2	3	2	3	3	2	23
7	Denmark	0	1	3	2	3	2	3	3	2	19
8	Estonia	2	2	3	2	3	2	3	3	2	22
9	Finland	2	1	2	2	3	2	2	3	3	20
10	France	2	2	3	2	3	2	3	3	2	22
11	Germany	1	2	3	2	3	2	2	3	2	20
12	Greece	0	3	3	2	3	3	3	3	2	22
13	Hungary	2	3	3	2	3	3	3	3	2	24
14	Ireland	1	2	3	2	3	3	3	3	2	22
15	Italy	2	3	3	3	3	3	3	3	2	25
16	Latvia	2	2	3	2	3	3	3	3	2	23
17	Lithuania	2	1	3	2	3	2	3	3	2	21
18	Luxembourg	2	2	2	2	2	3	3	3	2	21
19	Malta	2	3	3	2	3	3	3	3	2	24
20	Netherlands	0	2	3	2	2	2	3	3	2	19
21	Poland	1	3	3	2	3	3	3	3	2	23
22	Portugal	2	3	3	2	3	3	2	3	2	23
23	Romania	2	3	3	2	2	3	3	3	2	23
24	Slovakia	2	3	3	2	3	2	3	3	2	23
25	Slovenia	1	2	3	2	3	2	3	3	2	21
26	Spain	2	3	3	2	3	3	3	3	2	24
27	Sweden	0	1	1	1	2	1	1	1	1	9
28	United Kingdom	0	2	3	2	3	3	3	3	2	21

Source: Own study.

the maximum score of 26 and 27 points which allowed us to establish an internal typology. Thus, even the restrictive dimension of a state's policy may have its variations. For the purpose of this book, an internal typology of state policy was made into: significantly restrictive policy and moderately restrictive policy. In the first case, the score is determined by GPCI = 22–27 points and in the second case, GPCI = 19–21 points. This procedure allowed us to distinguish between countries whose policies were definitely restrictive (Austria, Belgium, Bulgaria, Republic of Cyprus, the Czech Republic, Estonia, France, Greece, Hungary, Ireland, Italy, Latvia, Malta, Poland,

Portugal, Romania, Slovakia, and Spain) and countries which did not take such radical actions (Croatia, Denmark, Finland, Germany, Lithuania, Luxembourg, the Netherlands, Slovenia, and the United Kingdom). Denmark, the Netherlands, and Finland scored the lowest in their GPCI group with 19, 19, and 20 points, respectively, being very close to the border with the score for medium policy.

Notes

1 The research also includes Great Britain, as it was one of the member states of the European Union during the period under study.
2 The initial assumption was to conduct research using a research tool Governments Effectiveness COVID Index [GECI], which would verify the effectiveness of the introduced solutions/restrictions in the EU countries. Thus, the correlation between the restrictions applied by the countries and the effects of their application (i.e. the number of diseases and the number of deaths) was established. The process of conducting the research made it possible to verify that the assumptions made in the book project had some kind of errors and that viewed in that way, it is not possible to establish the correlation. First of all, the daily incidence number is significantly distorted because it depends on the number of COVID-19 tests performed in a given state. It was a characteristic of most states that the number of tests performed changed (with an increase or decrease in incidence). It is not possible to verify from this how the restrictions implied on the flattening of the incidence curve. Secondly, the mortality figures are also difficult to relate to the effectiveness of the state policy towards COVID-19, since, for example, the closure of service premises, or the introduction of limits in stores or public transport, has no direct impact on mortality. Much more objective, in this case, the causal factor seems to be the quality of the Health Service.
3 All variables X are treated as equivalent; the paper does not undertake the task of assigning them special weight for a given catalogue. The reason for this is that some variables may be perceived with different intensities in many countries. So, to avoid distorting the model, gradations of variables were used.
4 The creation of the nominal measurement scale for the GPCI was based on three challenges: conceptualisation, measurement, and aggregation. Thus, it involved operationalising and establishing government policy variables relative to COVID-19, selecting X attributes, and establishing gradations. (Sulek, 2010, pp. 91–94; Munck & Verkuilen, 2002, pp. 7–27; Szewczak, 2012, pp. 45–68).
5 Each state individually established a list of these countries.

References

Act on Security Regions. (2020). *Wet veiligheidsregio's*. https://wetten.overheid.nl/BWBR0027466/2020-01-01
Acts of legislative content. (2020). Νόμος v. ΠΝΠ25.02.2020/2020 Πράξη Νομοθετικού Περιεχομένου της 25.02.2020 Κατεπείγοντα μέτρα αποφυγής και περιορισμού της διάδοσης κορωνοϊού www.taxheaven.gr/law/%CE%A0%CE%9D%CE%A025.02.2020/2020

Alto Comissariado para as Migrações. (2021). *COVID-19: Measures, guidelines and recommendations.* https://www.acm.gov.pt/en/68?p_p_id=101&p_p_lifecycle= 0&p_p_state=maximized&p_p_mode=view&_101_struts_action=%2Fasset_ publisher%2Fview_content&_101_assetEntryId=779537&_101_type=content&_ 101_urlTitle=covid-19-medidas-orientacoes-e-recomendacoes

Austria Covid Act. (2020). *Consolidated federal law: Entire legal provision for COVID-19 Measures Act, version of April 29, 2020.*

Austrian Federal Ministry for Social Affairs. (n.d.). *Health, care and consumer protection. Nationwide measures.* https://corona-ampel.gv.at/aktuelle-massnahmen/ bundesweite-massnahmen/

Bayer, L., & Cokeleare, H. (2020, March). *The EU travel ban explained: Governments force commission into U-turn over fears it was moving too quickly, Politico EU, 17.* www.politico.eu/article/the-eu-european-union-coronavirus

Belgian Federal Public Service. (n.d.). *Health, food chain safety and environment. Face masks. I protect you, you protect me.* www.info-coronavirus.be/en/ facemask/

Belgium. COVID-19 (I). (2020a). Loi habilitant le Roi à prendre des mesures de lutte contre la propagation du coronavirus COVID-19 (I), No 1104/5.\ http://www.ilo. org/dyn/natlex/natlex4.detail?p_lang=&p_isn=110383&p_count=106443&p_ classification=01.08&p_classcount=104

Belgium, COVID-19 (II). (2020b). Loi habilitant le Roi à prendre des mesures de lutte contre la propagation du coronavirus COVID-19 (II), No 1104/6. http://www.ilo. org/dyn/natlex/natlex4.detail?p_lang=&p_isn=110383&p_count=106443&p_ classification=01.08&p_classcount=104

Bulgaria travel advice. (n.d). www.gov.uk/foreign-travel-advice/bulgaria/coronavirus

Bulgaria. Health System Response Monitor. (2021). *COVID-19.* www.covid19 healthsystem.org/countries/bulgaria/livinghit.aspx?Section=1.1%20Health%20 communication&Type=Section

Colfer, B. (2020). Herd-immunity across intangible borders: Public policy responses to COVID-19 in Ireland and the UK. *European Policy Analysis, 6*(2).

Coronavirus Act UK. (2020). www.legislation.gov.uk/ukpga/2020/7/contents/enacted

Coronavirus pandemic in the EU. (2020). *Fundamental rights implications, bulletin #1.* https://fra.europa.eu/sites/default/files/fra_uploads/fra-2020-coronavirus-pandemic-eu-bulletin_en.pdf

Covid-19 in Greece. (2020). https://phmovement.org/covid-19-in-greece/

Croatia introduces new measures. (2020). Masks mandatory in all closed spaces, restrictions imposed on gatherings. *Croatiaweek.* www.croatiaweek.com/croatia-introduces-new-measures-masks-mandatory-in-all-closed-spaces-restrictions-imposed-on-gatherings/

Coronavirus in Croatia. (2021). www.koronavirus.hr/en

Cyprus. (2020). *Adopts mask-wearing outdoors to contain virus spike.* https://medical xpress.com/news/2020-10-cyprus-mask-wearing-outdoors-virus-spike.html

Czech Republic, Crisis Act. (2000). No. 240/2000 Coll (krizový zákon č. 240/2000 Sb.). https://www.zakonyprolidi.cz/cs/2000-240

Danish Health Authority. (n.d.). *Covid-19 information.* www.sst.dk/en/English/ Corona-eng

Danish Ministry of Health. (n.d.). *COVID-19 lockdown.* https://en.coronasmitte.dk/rules-and-regulations

Decisions and guidelines in the Ministry of Health and Social Affairs'. (2020). *Policy areas to limit the spread of the COVID-19 virus.* www.government.se/articles/2020/04/s-decisions-and-guidelines-in-the-ministry-of-health-and-social-affairs-policy-areas-to-limit-the-spread-of-the-covid-19-virusny-sida/

Declaration of a Public Health Emergency Order. (2020). https://legislation.mt/eli/ln/2020/115/eng/pdf

Declaration of Emergency Situation. (2020). *In the administrative territory of the Republic of Estonia.* www.riigiteataja.ee/en/eli/ee/VV/k/524042020008/consolide

Decree of the President of the Republic Portugal. (2020). No 14-A/2020 of 18 March 2020, Diário da República, 1st Series, No 55. https://dre.pt/dre/LinkAntigo?search=130399862

The Decree of the President of Romania. (2020). no. 195 / 16.03.2020 on the establishment of the state of emergency on the territory of Romania. *Official Gazette of Romania, Part I.*

Department of Foreign Affairs of Italy. (2021). www.dfa.ie/travel/travel-advice/a-z-list-of-countries/italy/

Epidemic Act of Denmark. (2019). *Covid Bekendtgørelse af lov om foranstaltninger mod smitsomme og andre overførbare sygdomm, LBK nr 1026 af 01/10/2019.* www.retsinformation.dk/eli/lta/2019/1026

Estonian Government. (n.d.). www.kriis.ee/en?destination=/en&_exception_status code=404

European Commission. (2020, March 16). *Communication from the commission to the European Parliament, the European Council and the Council, COVID-19: Temporary restriction on non-essential travel to the EU, COM(2020) 115 final.* https://ec.europa.eu/transparency/regdoc/rep/1/2020/EN/COM-2020-115-F1-EN MAIN-PART-1.PDF

Federal Constitutional Law of Austria. (2021), *Entire legal provision for the Federal Constitutional Act, version dated November 7th, 2021.* www.ris.bka.gv.at/GeltendeFassung.wxe?Abfrage=Bundesnormen&Gesetzesnummer=10000138

Federal Ministry of Health Republic of Austria. (n.d.). *COVID-19 information.* www.sozialministerium.at/en/Coronavirus/New-coronavirus-(COVID-19).html

Federal Ministry of Health. Germany. (n.d.). www.zusammengegencorona.de/en/?articlefilter=all

Federal Public Service, Belgium. (n. d.). *COVID-19 information.* www.health.belgium.be/en/covid-19-temporary-authorisations

Fiinland Stafe of Emergency. (2020). https://valtioneuvosto.fi/-/10616/hallitus-totesi-suomen-olevan-poikkeusoloissa-koronavirustilanteen-vuoksi?languageId=en_US

Finland. (n.d.). *Recommendation on the use of face masks for citizens.* https://thl.fi/en/web/infectious-diseases-and-vaccinations/what-s-new/coronavirus-covid-19-latest-updates/transmission-and-protection-coronavirus/recommendation-on-the-use-of-face-masks-for-citizens

French Ordinance. (2020). *n°2020–306 of March 25,2020 adapts administrative proceeding during the state of public health emergency.*

Germany, the Infectious Diseases Protection Act. (2020). (Infektionsschutzgesetz, IfSG), https://perma.cc/B27B-36HD

The Governing Mayor of Berlin. (2021). *Senate Chancellery Corona virus information (Covid-19)*. www.berlin.de/corona/en/measures/

Governement de France. (n.d.). *Informations coronavirus*. www.gouvernement.fr/info-coronavirus

Government of Ireland. (n.d.). *COVID-19 information*. www.gov.ie/en/campaigns/c36c85-covid-19-coronavirus/

Government of Latvia. (n.d.). *COVID-19 FAQ*. https://covid19.gov.lv/en/covid-19-frequently-askedquestions-and-answers

Government of the Czech Republic. (2020). *The declaration of a state of emergency – updates on current measures* (Vyhlášení nouzového stavu – co aktuálně platí), press release 30 April 2020.

Government of the Czech Republic. (2021). *Measures adopted by the Czech Government against the coronavirus*. www.vlada.cz/en/media-centrum/aktualne/measures-adopted-by-the-czech-government-against-coronavirus-180545/2020

Government of the Netherlands. (n.d.). *Face masks mandatory in all indoor public spaces*. www.government.nl/topics/coronavirus-covid-19/

Government of the Republic of Croatia. (2020). https://vlada.gov.hr/coronavirus-protection-measures/28950

The Government of the Republic of Lithuania. (2020). *Resolution "on declaration of state-level emergency", No. 152 on 2020 February 26*. Valid from 2020 February 26 (Lietuvos Respublikos Vyriausybės 2020 m. vasario 26 d. Nr. 152 „Dėl valstybės lygio ekstremalios sistuacijos paskelbimo").

Government Resolution. (2020, 15 March). *No. 114/2020 on the proposal to declare state of emergency pursuant to the law no. 227/2002 Coll..´*. Retrieved from https://rokovania.gov.sk/RVL/Resolution/18252/1

Government UK. (n.d.). *Coronavirus*. www.gov.uk/coronavirus

Greece. National Public Health Organization. (2021). https://eody.gov.gr/en/covid-19/

Hale, T., Anania. J., Angrist., N., & all. (2021). Variation in government responses to COVID-19 Version 12.0. *Blavatnik School of Government Working Paper*. www.bsg.ox.ac.uk/research/publications/variation-government-responses-covid-19.

Hantrais, L., & Letablier, M. T. (2021). *Comparing and contrasting the impact of the COVID-19 pandemic in the European Union*. Routledge.

Hirsch, C. (2020). Europe's coronavirus lockdown measures compared. *Politico* EU, 15 April 2020. www.politico.eu/article/europes-coronavirus-lockdown

Hungary, Governmental Decision. (2020). no. 1102/2020. *On introducing a new work order in the public education institutions due to the coronavirus* (1102/2020. (III. 14.). Korm. határozat a koronavírus miatt a köznevelési és szakképzési intézményekben új munkarend bevezetéséről). http://njt.hu/cgi_bin/njt_doc.cgi?docid=218513.380693

Hungary, Governmental Decree. (2020, 11 March). *No. 40/2020. on declaring state of danger* (40/2020. (III. 11.). Korm. rendelet veszélyhelyzet kihirdetéséről). Retrieved from https://net.jogtar.hu/jogszabaly?docid=A2000040.KOR.

Hungary. Health System Response Monitor. (2021). *COVID-19*. www.covid19health
system.org/countries/hungary/livinghit.aspx?section=5.%20Governance&
Type=Chapter

The Infectious Diseases Protection Act. (2020). *Odluku o proglašenju zakona o
izmjenama i dopunama zakona o zaštiti pučanstva od zaraznih bolesti, 31/2020*.
https://narodne novine.nn.hr/clanci/sluzbeni/2020_04_47_954.html

IOM Migration Information Centre. (2021). *COVID-19: Official measures and
important information (updated continually)*. www.mic.iom.sk/en/news/637-
covid-19-measures.html

Iosa. M., Paolucci, S., & Morone G. (2020). Covid-19: A dynamic analysis of
fatality risk in Italy. *Frontiers in Medicine*, *7*(185). https://doi.org/10.3389/
fmed.2020.00185

Ireland Emergency Act. (2020). *Measures in the public interest (Covid-19)*.

Ireland Health Act. (2020). *Preservation and protection and other emergency
measures in the public interest*. https://www.irishstatutebook.ie/eli/2020/act/1/
enacted/en/html

Italian Republic Constitution. (1947). http://biblioteka.sejm.gov.pl/konstytucje-swiata-
wlochy/?lang=en

Jonung, L. (2020). *Sweden's constitution decides its exceptional Covid-19 policy*. https://
voxeu.org/article/sweden-s-constitution-decides-its-exceptional-covid-19-policy.

Karlson, N., Stern, Ch., & Klein, D. (2020). *The underpinnings of Sweden's permissive COVID regime*. https://voxeu.org/article/underpinnings-sweden-s-permissive-
covid-regime

Karolinska Institutet. (2020). https://news.ki.se/cloth-face-masks-can-reduce-the-
spread-of-sars-cov-2

La Constitution Belge. (2019). www.senate.be/doc/const_fr.html

Law on Measures and Actions during the State of Emergency. (2020). *Announced by
a decision of the National Assembly of March 13, 2020*. https://dv.parliament.bg/
DVWeb/showMaterialDV.jsp?idMat=147150

Legislation Mandatory Use of Medical or Cloth Masks. (2020). https://legislation.
mt/eli/ln/2020/402/eng/pdf

Lithuania. Department of Foreign Affairs. (2021). www.dfa.ie/travel/travel-advice/a-
z-list-of-countries/lithuania/

Luxembourg, Grand-ducal decree. (2020). *Of 18 March 2020 introducing a series of
measures to combat the Covid-19* (Règlement grand-ducal du 18 mars 2020 portant
introduction d'une série de mesures dans le cadre de la lutte contre le Covid-19).

Luxembourg. COVID-19 information. (n.d.). https://covid19.public.lu/en/sanitary-
measures/gatherings.html

Luyten, J., & Schokkaert, E. (2021). Belgium's response to the COVID-19 pandemic.
Health Economics Policy and Law, 17(1), 1–22. Doi:10.1017/S1744133121000232.

Ministry of Health Cyprus. (n.d.). www.moh.gov.cy/moh/moh.nsf/All/B61D53E79
B2D75E9C225851B003D33C7

Ministry of Health Italy. (n.d.). *COVID-19 information*. www.salute.gov.it/portale/
nuovocoronavirus/homeNuovoCoronavirus.jsp?lingua=english

Ministry of Health of Czech Republic. (n.d.). https://koronavirus.mzcr.cz/en/

The Ministry of Health. Latvia. (2021). *COVID-19 information*. www.vm.gov.lv/lv/aktualitates-par-covid-19

The Ministry of Health. Lithuania. (2021). *COVID-19 information*. https://sam.lrv.lt/en/

Ministry of Health Poland. (n.d.). *COVID-19 information*. www.gov.pl/web/zdrowie/covid

Ministry of Health, Consumer Affairs and Social Welfare. Spain. (n.d.). www.mscbs.gob.es/en/home.htm

Ministry of Health, Welfare and Sport, Netherlands. (2021). *COVID-19 information*. www.government.nl/ministries/ministry-of-health-welfare-and-sport/news/2021/09/03/changes-regarding-high-risk-and-very-high-risk-areas

Ministry of Health. Luxemburg. (n.d.). *COVID-19 information*. https://msan.gouvernement.lu/en/actualites.gouvernement%2Ben%2Bactualites%2Btoutes_actualites%2Bcommuniques%2B2021%2B11-novembre%2B10-retrospective.html

Ministry of Health. Malta. (n.d.). *COVID-19 information*. https://deputyprimeminister.gov.mt/en/health-promotion/covid-19/Pages/mitigation-conditions-and-guidances.aspx

Ministry of Health. Portugal. (n.d.). *COVID-19 information*. https://covid19.min-saude.pt/

Ministry of Health. Romania. (n.d.). *COVID-19 information*. www.ms.ro/-19.ebscomedical.com/ministry-health-romania

Ministry of Health. Slovakia. (n.d.). *COVID-19 information*. www.health.gov.sk/Titulka

Ministry of Health. Slovenia. (n.d.). *COVID-19 information*. www.gov.si/en/state-authorities/ministries/ministry-of-health/

Ministry of Social Affairs and Health. Finland. (2021). *COVID-19 information*. https://stm.fi/en/-/10616/government-adopts-plan-to-lift-covid-19-restrictions

Munck, G. L., & Verkuilen, J. (2002). Conceptualizing and measuring democracy: Evaluating alternative indices. *Comparative Political Studies, 35*, 1.

Odredba o razglasitvi epidemije nalezljive bolezni SARS-CoV-2 (COVID-19) (2020). *na območju Republike Slovenije*. www.pisrs.si/Pis.web/pregledPredpisa?id=ODRE2550.

The Official Development Agency of the City of Vilnius. (2021). *COVID-19: Covid-19 information*. www.govilnius.lt/media-news/important-information-regarding-the-coronavirus

The Oxford Coronavirus Government Response Tracker. (2021). www.bsg.ox.ac.uk/research/research-projects/covid-19-government-response-tracker

Portugal. Covid-19 information. (2021). https://covid19.min-saude.pt/ https://covid19.min-saude.pt/

Public Health Act of Netherlands. (2020). *Wet publieke gezondheid*. https://wetten.overheid.nl/BWBR0024705/2020-03-19

Public Health Agency of Sweden. (n.d.). www.folkhalsomyndigheten.se/the-public-health-agency-of-sweden/communicable-disease-control/covid-19/

Quarantine law – decree. UK. chapter 260, 2020. https://www.legislation.gov.uk/coronavirus

Regarding Declaration of the Emergency Situation. (2020). https://likumi.lv/ta/en/en/id/313191

Report Finland. (2020). *Coronavirus pandemic in the EU – Fundamental rights implications. e European Union Agency for Fundamental Rights (FRA).* https://fra.europa.eu/sites/default/files/fra_uploads/fi_report_on_coronavirus_pandemic_june_2020.pdf

Report Sweden. (2020). *Coronavirus pandemic in the EU – Fundamental rights implications. e European Union Agency for Fundamental Rights (FRA).* https://fra.europa.eu/sites/default/files/fra_uploads/sweden-report-covid-19-april-2020_en.pdf,

The Response Measures Database. (n.d.). https://covid-statistics.jrc.ec.europa.eu/RMeasures

Royal Decree. (2020). *463/2020, declaring the state of alarm for the management of the health crisis situation caused by COVID-19 in Spain.* https://www.osborneclarke.com/insights/main-measures-established-royal-decree-4632020-14-march-declaring-state-alarm-management-health-crisis-situation-caused-covid-19

Rozporządzenie Ministra Zdrowia. (2020). *z dnia 20 marca 2020 r. w sprawie ogłoszenia na obszarze Rzeczypospolitej Polskiej stanu epidemii.* https://sip.lex.pl/akty-prawne/dzu-dziennik-ustaw/ogloszenie-na-obszarze-rzeczypospolitej-polskiej-stanu-epidemii-18972567

Spain State of Alarm. (2020). *eal Decreto 463/2020, de 14 de marzo, por el que se declara el estado de alarma para la gestión de la situación de crisis sanitaria ocasionada por el COVID-19.* https://boe.es/buscar/act.php?id=BOE-A-2020-3692

Statistica. (2021). *Cumulative number of coronavirus.* www.statista.com/statistics/1102896/coronavirus-cases-development-europe/

Stringency Index. (2021). https://ourworldindata.org/grapher/covid-stringency-index

Sulek, M. (2010). *Prognozowanie i symulacje międzynarodowe.* SHOLAR.

Swedish-Government. Strategy in response to the COVID-19 pandemic. (2020). www.government.se/articles/2020/04/strategy-in-response-to-the-covid-19-pandemic/. Accessed September 1, 2021

Szewczak, W. (2012). Budowanie skali pomiarowej w politologii. *Athenaeum. Polskie Studia Politologiczne, 36.*

UK Department of Health and Social Care. (n.d.). *COVID-19 information.* www.gov.uk/government/organisations/department-of-health-and-social-care

UK Government Department for Education. (2020). www.gov.uk/government/organisations/department-for-education

Website of the Republic of Poland. (n.d.). *Coronavirus: Information and recommendations.* www.gov.pl/web/coronavirus/temporary-limitations

WHO. (2021). *Global research on coronavirus disease (Covid-19).* www.who.int/emergencies/diseases/novel-coronavirus-2019/global-research-on-novel-coronavirus-2019-ncov

World Bank. (2020). *People density-Belgium.* Retrieved from https://data.worldbank.org/indicator/EN.POP.DNST?locations=BE.

2 European societies and their behaviour towards coronavirus

Magdalena Tomala

Introduction

Identifying pandemic situations is one of the key tasks of state authorities that manage health policy and other key areas of the economy. These actions are aimed at avoiding, preventing, and counteracting the surprise caused by a crisis situation (Andrzejewski, 2010, p. 163). Much depends on how the authorities organise and manage the pandemic to avoid losses associated with increased mortality, as well as the economy, exposed to slowdown. On the other hand, one cannot overlook the role of the society in this aspect; how it will behave in a different, unusual situation, for which so far there had been no set rules, norms, or laws. In these specific, exceptional conditions, therefore, the cooperation of the two parties, i.e. the state and society, is of key importance, including adherence to a sanitary regime by people or acceptance of vaccinations. It should be emphasised that this shared responsibility not only for oneself but also for others will promote the effectiveness of pandemic control, while the attitude of the population in individualistic type states may contribute to the aggravation of the crisis.

The aim of Chapter 2 is to examine the relationship between the social capital of European countries and effective management during a pandemic. The year 2020, which was entirely dominated by pandemic management, is examined. It can be hypothesised that a society with high social capital should perform better in managing during a pandemic. The independent variable in this case will be the value of social capital, while the dependent variable, showing the effectiveness of management, will be: the level of vaccination of the population, the number of confirmed cases of COVID-19, the mortality resulting from COVID-19, and the number of people subjected to hospitalisation.

Chapter 2 of the study consists of three parts. The first one analyses the literature on social research conducted during the pandemic. The next step was to examine the effectiveness of the fight against COVID-19. For this

DOI: 10.4324/9781003222538-2

purpose, the correlation between the dependent variable (mortality during the pandemic) and the independent variable (social capital) was examined. This analysis will provide an answer to the question of the existence of a relationship between social capital and the spread of COVID-19 in the countries under examination. The third part examines the features of social capital of the European Union countries in terms of compliance with laws and social norms and the features that shape cooperative or individualistic attitudes during the pandemic.

2.1 Research on social capital during the pandemic caused by COVID-19 virus

The COVID-19 pandemic situation is an unusual phenomenon. The novelty, the unfamiliarity with the methods of fighting the virus contributes to the lack of appropriate action by states, multiplied by the absence of proven solutions that rulers could apply, confident of the effectiveness of their decisions. Extremely useful in this aspect is the literature, analysing the effectiveness of the actions of various actors in the world, including medical, state, or institutional ones. The onset of the pandemic revealed deficiencies in this area, but researchers have begun to fill the gaps by analysing subsequent waves of the epidemic. In the period from 2019 to 2021, more than 4 million search terms related to COVID-19 could be found on Google Scholar. This demonstrates the great interest in the topic, the need to find answers to a number of questions on medical as well as social aspects related to the spread of the COVID-19 together with management strategies during the pandemic.

In turn, the question of analysing the role of social capital in the fight against COVID-19 has so far more than 350,000 records. This means that researchers assign important roles to social capital, determining the effectiveness of emergency management actors. It is worth noting that the need for research on COVID-19, including non-medical ways to combat the pandemic, has resulted in the emergence of various social science competitions. Many countries and organisations around the world have taken up the challenge of finding innovative ways to overcome the COVID-19 crisis, the most important being the WHO, which "is bringing the world's scientists and global health professionals together to accelerate the research and development process, and develop new norms and standards to contain the spread of the coronavirus pandemic and help care for those affected" (WHO, 2021b). The most important goal of the research being undertaken was the invention of a vaccine. Experts convinced the public that a high percentage of the population being vaccinated (more than 80%) would allow to combat the pandemic. Research began on January 11, 2020, and the first prototypes, ready for clinical trials were ready as early as March 2020. The most advanced work concerns vaccine preparations: mRNA vaccines, vector vaccines, and recombinant protein vaccines with adjuvants. Two vaccine types have been approved for marketing within the European Union, including Pfizer and BioNTech's mRNA vaccine, Moderna's mRNA vaccine, Astra Zeneca's vector vaccine developed in collaboration with Oxford University, and Janssen's vector vaccine (WHO, 2021a).

Among the countries involved in research on COVID-19 were not only the largest economies like the United States (National Institutes of Health, 2021) but also smaller countries such as Poland, which under the slogan "Science against Covid" (Narodowe Centrum Nauki, 2020) announced a competition named *Fast Track access to funds for research on COVID-19*. It is worth noting that the aforementioned entities studied not only medical aspects but also social issues in combating the pandemic.

Within the European Union, social science research was included in comprehensive studies within the RECOVER work packages. These aimed to analyse the social and behavioural experiences of patients and physicians in providing and receiving care during the COVID-19 pandemic, including understanding risk perceptions, public trust in health professionals, governments, science, public willingness to participate in clinical trials, and others (European Commission, 2021).

The COVID-19 research activities undertaken have resulted in numerous scientific publications. Most of these were medical in nature, including diagnosis (Weissleder et al., 2020), prevention (Watkins, 2020), or vaccine research (Thanh Le et al., 2020) and others.

The authors attempted to analyse the relationship between social capital and medical issues. In revealing the role of social capital in combating COVID-19, they highlighted different aspects of this relationship.

First, the research articles analysed the social consequences of the pandemic. One of the most frequently raised social issues related to restrictions on free movement and lockdown was isolation and its consequences, including but not limited to loneliness. For example, Amy Rachel Bland and co-authors examined the effects of COVID-19 social isolation on aspects of emotional and social cognitive function. The authors hypothesised that greater impairment in emotional and social cognitive function would be observed in individuals who experienced greater disruptions in their usual social connectivity during COVID-19 social isolation (Bland et al., 2021, pp. 1–10). In contrast, Na Li and co-authors examined risk factors for psychiatric disorders after the COVID-19 outbreak and tested the possible mediating role of social support and emotional intelligence in the relationship between exposure to COVID-19 pandemic and psychiatric disorders. They positively verified the hypothesis and hence concluded that psychological interventions to support emotional intelligence and social support should be implemented among university students to reduce psychological damage caused by COVID-19 pandemic (Li et al., 2021, pp. 1–9). It is important to note that the issues of remote education and remote work have been widely discussed in the literature. Using survey methods, the authors examined the psychological consequences of isolation as well as social adjustment to a changing environment.

Second, researchers have also emphasised the importance of trust in authority, including the role of community capacity, which contributes significantly to the success of the fight against COVID-19. For example, Hartley and Jarvis analysed how "community capacity underpinned Hong Kong's early success in responding to the COVID-19 crisis" (Hartley & Jarvis, 2020, p. 404). According to them, the success of management is evidenced by the low number of confirmed cases, the limited number of hospitalisations due to COVID-19, and the mortality rate, which should take into account non-medical methods to combat the pandemic like isolation, quarantine, and adherence to guidelines including wearing masks. The issue of trust was also analysed by Cairney and Wellstead using US and UK examples, indicating that three elements are important in effective pandemic management: "policy-makers trust in experts to help them understand the policy problem, policy-makers trust in citizens to follow government advice or instruction, and public trust in government and government policy" (Cairney & Wellstead, 2020, p. 2). When dealing with the non-medical aspects of crisis management, there exist three main actors: government, citizens, and experts whose relationships with each other determine success. The issue of trust during a pandemic has also been addressed by other researchers, such as (Elgar et al., 2020, pp. 1–6); (Dohle et al., 2020, pp. 1–23); (Bourguignon & Sprenger, 2021, pp. 2–3).

Third, an interesting approach to social capital is presented by Cappello and Rizzuto, who emphasise the importance of disinformation or fake news, through which "it is no longer possible to separate reality from media reconstruction of reality" (Cappello & Rizzuto, 2020, p. 4). More specifically, the issues of disinformation are addressed by Bharathidasan, who analyses the discussion on the usefulness of wearing masks during the COVID-19 pandemic. The problem, they point out, demonstrates the efficiency of state action in a crisis. It contributes to the balance between business and the situation requiring lockdown.

Central to this paper are the results of studies that have considered the role of social capital in combating pandemics. Of note is a paper in which the authors, using anonymised travel records of COVID-19 patients (this study examines the effect of social capital on individuals' responses to control measures early in the COVID-19 pandemic in China), show that social capital as measured by social trust, media coverage of social norms, and public recognition of social norms has a significant effect on reducing individuals' common catalogue of solutions cover the mouth and nose behaviour. Mechanism tests showed that social capital reduces the prevalence of close contact behaviour by encouraging people to follow public morality, which refers to self-control during quarantine. Deeper analysis showed that social trust does not show a significant effect on all entertainment activities and that media coverage of social norms is more conducive to preventing family entertainment than a public acceptance of social norms. Moreover, improving public acceptance of social norms plays a decisive role in preventing social entertainment. This study sheds important light on the crucial role that informal institutions play in epidemic prevention and control (Liu & Wen, 2021, pp. 1–11). Among the numerous articles focused on social capital during pandemic outbreaks, a paper in which the authors used county-level data from the United States to document the role of social capital in the evolution of COVID-19 between January 2020 and January 2021 is also noteworthy. They noted that social capital differences in COVID-19-related deaths and hospitalisations depend on social capital, but the time frame of the pandemic is important. Communities with higher levels of relational and cognitive social capital were decidedly more effective in reducing COVID-19-related deaths and hospitalisations from late March to early April than communities with lower social capital. A difference of one standard deviation in relational social capital corresponded to a 30% reduction in the number of recorded COVID-19-related deaths. In contrast, differences in COVID-19-related deaths associated with relational social capital persisted in subsequent waves of the crisis, i.e. after April 2020, although they gradually became less pronounced. In contrast, during the March–April 2020 period, estimates indicated that there was no statistically significant difference in the number of deaths recorded in areas with different levels of cognitive social capital. In fact, from late June to early July, the number of COVID-19-related new deaths was higher in communities with higher levels of cognitive social capital. The total number of deaths recorded between January 2020 and January 2021 was lower in communities with higher levels of relational social capital (Borgonovi et al., 2021, pp. 1–12). In addition, researchers Francesca Borgonovi and Elodie Andrieu also examined the level of mobility, and mobility focused on commercial and recreational activities (Borgonovi & Andrieu, 2020, pp. 1–12).

Research was also conducted to analyse the role of social capital in mitigating mental health harm caused by social or mobility constraints. The authors tested levels of mental stress during a pandemic as well as mitigating the harm of social/mobility constraints. Findings showed that at the individual level, social capital was associated with less psychological stress. As a result, increasing restrictions had a weaker effect on the stress of individuals who thus interacted more frequently with their neighbours (Laurence & Kim, 2021, pp. 1–29).

In conclusion, it is important to emphasise the variety of methods and tools that the researchers used. The limitations that the researchers faced also play a role. The most important problem was the limited access to data, which is important especially for comparative analysis at the international level. Often the researchers were limited to analysing the situation in one selected country, less frequently the research concerned a group of countries or was of global character. Another problem is the variety of research methods used to measure social capital, which contributed to the lack of homogeneity of results. It should also be noted that the authors mentioned other additional factors that influenced the research results (weather, administrative measures, etc.). Despite these barriers, it should be noted that the conclusions of the study can provide valuable guidance to decision makers in countries around the world. They allow to implement an appropriate strategy of action and to stimulate the behaviour of communities in the next waves of the pandemic, should they come.

2.2 Social responsibility during COVID-19 pandemic

A pandemic is an extremely unique situation because it occurs infrequently and there are no specific procedures for dealing with such situations. The term comes from the Greek (*pan* – "all," *demos* – "people, populace") and denotes an epidemic of some disease occurring worldwide, on different continents, in many countries. Most often we are dealing with infectious diseases that spread easily among people. In the previous century, pandemics were mainly caused by influenza viruses, with the Spanish flu pandemic in 1918–1920 being one of the largest and most dangerous pandemics. It is estimated that about 500 million people fell ill, i.e. about one-third of the world's population at that time, and between 20 million and 50 million people died, according to various estimates. In addition, there were two more pandemics in the 20th century: the Asian flu and the Hong-Kong flu.

The lack of established rules of conduct contributes to the situation that both the rulers in a given country and the society behave intuitively or even randomly. The question can be asked about the effectiveness of the actions of these actors during a pandemic. This section focuses on the social dimension, that is, on social responsibility and its impact on the effectiveness of the fight against COVID-19. To this end, the correlation between the independent variable (social capital) and the dependent variables (mortality, hospitalisations, vaccinations, and confirmed cases of COVID-19 in each country) was examined.

2.2.1   Social capital – defining the problem

The independent variable, i.e. social capital, defines those features of social organisations, such as networks (arrangements) of individuals or households and their associated norms and values, that create externalities for the community as a whole (Putnam, 1995, pp. 65–78). This is one of many definitions in which Robert Putnam emphasised large communities because he believed that they had a greater impact on economic growth. In addition, he emphasised that the characteristics attributed to the term should be social trust and shared values that communities possess. However, the indicated elements are not sufficient to speak of the existence of social capital. According to him, social capital can only be observed when there are grassroots initiatives in a given society, which testify to the self-organising potential of a given group. It is nothing more than civic engagement, which manifests itself in the establishment of relationships, additional common quality, benefiting all members of the community (Putnam, 1995, pp. 65–78).

Nowadays, we are dealing with a multitude of definitions of social capital, its different interpretations, and many proposals for measuring the phenomenon itself. We can distinguish two schools here: one represented by Coleman, then continued by Robert Putnam and Francis Fukuyama, and the other represented by Pierre Bourdieu.

The first of the schools studying social capital is related to James Coleman, who in his work *Social Capital in the Creation of Human Capital* analysed the variation in school achievement due to individual predisposition – on the one hand, and the influence of school and family – on the other hand. He introduced the concept of social capital into the literature, defining it as a set of several components, that is, component variables such as trust, norms, and ties between people, improving their performance and facilitating the creation of a social community (Coleman, 1988, pp. 95–120). In addition, he defines the function of capital as serving collective action rather than solely the individual struggle of an actor in the social field. Social capital is productive because it allows certain goals to be achieved that would not be possible if it were lacking.

The Bourdieu School defines the concept of social capital differently. Bourdieu presents the concept of capital in terms of two terms, i.e. social field and habitus. Among the forms of capital, Bourdieu distinguishes: economic capital, i.e. money and material objects that can be used to produce products and services; cultural capital, i.e. skills, customs, habits, lifestyles; symbolic capital, which consists of symbols used to legitimise the possession of the other forms of capital; and social capital, which he defines as the sum of actual and potential resources that are due to an individual or group by virtue of having a durable, more or less institutionalised network of relationships, acquaintanceships, and mutual recognition (Bourdieu, 1986, pp. 15–29; Tittenbrun, 2016, pp. 81–103). Social capital in Bourdieu's view is a private good. The individual or collective benefits from it by functioning in fields. It has the ability to convert it, although there are many variables that determine the possibilities in this regard, ranging from the habitus of individuals to the logic of a given field. The potential of social capital at an actor's disposal depends on the field in which he participates, but also on his ability to mobilise it as determined by his habitus. Bourdieu does not specify the principles of capital conversion. In his opinion, it is not possible to unambiguously define the relationship between different forms of capitals. Their value in different fields may be different and not all of them will be valued equally in different fields. It depends on the logic of a particular field, which may change (Bourdieu & Wacquant, 2006, p. 659). Moreover, he views the functions of social capital, primarily, through the lens of social actors as its disposers who can make investments to increase the level of this capital. He differentiates social structure in both collective and individual aspects (Turner et al., 2004, p. 599).

The compilation of many definitions of social capital has resulted in the emergence of attempts to measure it. For the purpose of this article, the social capital measurement methodology prepared by SolAbility was used. It is a Swiss-Korean joint-venture company established in 2005 (*About Solability*, 2021). SolAbility is a sustainable intelligence think-tank and management consultancy. They designed and implemented sustainability strategies, policies, and management tools. They define social capital as: "the sum of social stability and the well-being (perceived or real) of the entire population. Social Capital generates social cohesion and a certain level of consensus, which in turn delivers a stable environment for the economy, and prevents natural resources from being over-exploited" (*Social Capital Index*, 2020). In measuring social capital, they include tools such as: health care systems and their universal availability/affordability (measuring physical health); income and asset equality, which are correlated to crime levels; demographic structure (to assess the future generational balance within a society); freedom of expression and freedom from fear; and the absence of violent conflicts. On this basis, it is possible to compare the incidence of social capital at the level of countries.

Therefore, it is worth considering how the issue of social capital in the EU countries looks in comparison to the world average and selected countries, as presented in Figure 2.1.

As the chart shows, capital in EU countries is at a high level. It differs by more than 10 points from the world average. Significant differences can also be noted in the case of Russia, Brazil, or the United States. This indicates the high potential of the EU as a group of countries integrating not only in trade

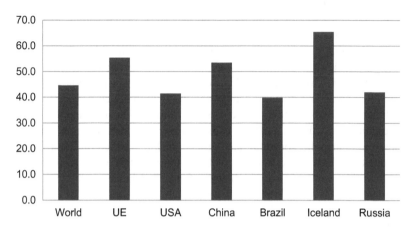

Figure 2.1 Social capital in the world in 2020

Source: Own study based on the data from *Social Capital Index* (2020).

but also in common values. This is also confirmed by the ranking positions of the individual EU countries in the social capital ranking. As many as five of the first ten places are occupied by EU countries, those include Sweden, Finland, Estonia, Austria, and Slovenia. Sweden is the highest ranked country, and Hungary is the lowest ranked of the EU countries with 68th place.

Putnam divides forms of social capital into formal and informal ones (Putnam, 2001, p. 42). The formal ones include initiatives such as associations, foundations, and others. Informal forms, on the other hand, can include community initiatives, often spontaneous or neighbourhood based. It is difficult to measure such initiatives due to their local character, but it is worth mentioning examples of such activities occurring in various EU countries. One of the first social initiatives – which appeared in Poland at the beginning of the epidemic and resulted from the lack of materials to protect the population – was the sewing of masks. These were distributed on the streets and taken to households and hospitals. Other examples included neighbourly help in shopping for quarantined people and assistance in buying medicines. One can also point to formal actions such as: legal assistance during the pandemic, resulting, for example, from job loss, and psychological assistance for families or children.

Recognising that in the EU countries there is a high level of social capital, one can consider the issue of its change over time, including changes under the influence of crisis situations. A pandemic should be a stimulus, an impulse to action for a community with a high level of social capital.

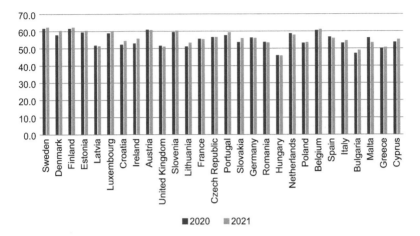

Figure 2.2 Comparison of social capital in the EU States in the years 2020 and 2021

Source: Own study based on the data from *Social Capital Index* (2020), *Social Capital Index* (2021).

On the other hand, the lack or low level of social capital may contribute to selfish, individual behaviour during a pandemic. Figure 2.2 presents the evolution of social capital in EU countries in 2020–2021, trying to answer the question whether social capital increased or decreased in EU countries during the pandemic. Considering the time frame, one could reach for the results of Borgonovi and Andrieu who pointed out the decreasing capital resulting from the prolonged crisis (Borgonovi et al., 2021; Borgonovi & Andrieu, 2020).

As shown in the chart, social capital has increased by 1 point on average in most EU countries over the study period. These are not large differences. The average for EU countries in 2020 equalled 55.4 points and in 2021 it stood at 55.98 points out of 100 possible. In turn, the median, dividing the collective of EU countries into two parts, was 56.19 in 2020 and 55.87 in 2021. Hungary has the minimum social capital for 2020 and 2021, while Sweden has the maximum. This means that the difference between the country with the lowest and highest social capital is in 2020–15.6 points and 16.6 points in 2021. The decrease of social capital took place in such countries as: Latvia, Austria, Great Britain, France, Germany, Romania, Hungary, the Netherlands, Spain, and Malta (the most – by as many as 2.7 points). On the other hand, the highest increase of social capital in this period was noted in Ireland (2.9 points).

In conclusion, social capital in the EU countries is at a fairly high level compared to other countries or the world average. We can confirm the hypothesis presented at the beginning that the crisis situation contributed to the growth of social capital in the studied countries. This indicates a positive response to the threat and allows us to conclude that during the pandemic there was social responsibility. It should be noted, however, that this conclusion should not be taken as a zero-sum game. It only indicates a trend that a large part of society respected norms and rules and responded positively to the threat. Therefore, it should be noted that although the conclusion indicates that the social capital is higher than the world average, its value is within the range of 50%–60% of possible points. This in turn allows us to conclude that only to a moderate degree can we expect the effectiveness of the fight against COVID-19.

2.2.2   *Pandemic management effectiveness in EU countries*

Given the importance of social capital in shaping norms and values in a country, it is worth taking a closer look at whether there is a relationship between social capital and pandemic management effectiveness. The following research hypotheses were adopted in this paper:

H1 – as social capital increases in a country, there is a reduction in the negative effects of a pandemic in the form of fewer illness cases;

H2 – as social capital increases in a country, there is a reduction in the negative effects of the pandemic in the form of reduced hospitalisations for COVID-19;

H3 – as social capital increases in a country, there is an increase in public vaccination against COVID-19;

H4 – as social capital increases in a country, there is a reduction in the negative effects of the pandemic in terms of reduced mortality.

All 28 countries, members of the EU, were included in the study. The UK withdrew from the EU during this period, but was part of the EU at some point during the pandemic, with implications in terms of freedom of movement.

The independent variable was social capital, measured by a scale adapted from the think-tank SolAbility. It produced the Social Capital ranking, one of the measurements of sustainable development, from 2020 to 2021. This tool comprises five components: health, equality, crime, freedom, and satisfaction, consisting of the following variables (cluster):

• Health: healthcare availability, child mortality, family planning;
• Equality: income equality, resource equality, gender equality;

- Crime: theft, violent crime, prison population;
- Freedom: press freedom, human rights, violent conflicts;
- Satisfaction: individual happiness, suicide rate.

The indicated variables form The Social Capital of a nation index defined as: the sum of social stability and the well-being (perceived or real) of the entire population and defined on a scale from 0 to 100 points (*Social Capital Index*, 2020).

The dependent variables were related to the effectiveness of management during the pandemic period. The first is the incidence rate of COVID-19, calculated as the number of tests performed in a country, i.e. cases – cumulative total per 100,000 population. The second variable is the number of fatal cases associated with COVID-19. The analysis of the first two variables used data made available by WHO and the number of vaccinations, measured as a percentage of the population (WHO, 2021b). The last variable concerns the number of hospitalisations due to COVID-19 (*Data on Hospital and ICU Admission Rates and Current Occupancy for COVID-19*, 2021). The database does not include data for Germany, Romania, and Greece.

To determine the direct relationships between the independent variable and the dependent variables, we look at the scatterplots of the independent variable with the dependent variables. Pearson correlation analysis was used to determine a relationship between the variables. The formula for the r-Pearson correlation coefficient has the form of

$$r(x, y) = cov(x, y)\sigma x * \sigma y$$

whereby

$$cov(x, y) = E(x * y) - (E(x) * E(y))$$

where:

$r(x, y)$ – Pearson correlation coefficient between variables x and y,
$cov(x, y)$ – covariance between variables x and y,
σ – standard deviation from the population,
E – expected value.

In order to establish direct relationships between the studied variables, as well as to verify hypotheses 1–4, correlation analysis was conducted. Table 2.1 presents the results of the study.

The analysis conducted sought to determine how social capital correlates with pandemic mitigation in the form of increased pandemic management effectiveness. The theoretical framework of the study was the Pearson correlation model. It shows that social capital is moderately associated with

Table 2.1 The relationship between research variables

Variables	Min.	1st Qu.	Median	Mean	3rd Qu.	Max.	Corelation with social capital
Hospitalisation	23.52	48.06	103.35	212.38	266.13	1156.07	−0.5454259
Total cases	28655	83347	107201	106464	126767	165188	0.06332064
Total deaths	210.9	1152.2	1751.0	1746.6	2250.6	3524.8	−0.5577285
Vaccination	0.2000	0.5046	0.6240	0.5970	0.6811	0.8585	0.4101294
Social Capital	46.03	53.01	56.19	55.43	58.80	61.65	1

Source: Own study.

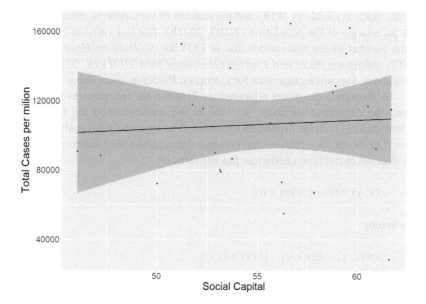

Figure 2.3 Scatterplot of social capital and cumulative total cases per million population
Source: Own study.

three dependent variables: i.e. number of hospitalisations, number of vaccinations, and COVID-19 mortality. Moreover, social capital correlates negatively with the number of hospitalisations on COVID-19 and mortality. In contrast, a positive correlation can be observed for vaccination.

As can be seen from the graph, the number of cases of COVID-19 does not correlate with the other variables such as social capital, mortality due to COVID-19, the number of hospitalisations, or the level of vaccination of the population (Figure 2.3).

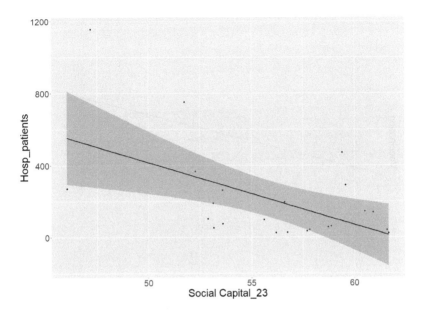

Figure 2.4 Scatterplot of social capital and hospitalisation per million population
Source: Own study.

Hypothesis H1, that with an increase in social capital there is a decrease in the incidence of COVID-19, could not be confirmed. The question arises why the relationship between the number of cases of COVID-19 and social capital was not verified positively. It can be assumed that in many countries, the number of ill people did not correspond to statistical values, due to underestimation of cases and inadequate population testing (more on this in Section 3).

In other cases, we were able to confirm the hypotheses. In the case of hypothesis H2, we can confirm that with an increase in social capital, we can observe a decrease in hospitalisations for COVID-19. Both variables are negatively associated with each other (see Figure 2.4).

In turn, social capital correlates positively with vaccination rates in EU countries (see Figure 2.5).

Thus, hypothesis H3 can be confirmed. That is, with the increase of social capital, the awareness of the population about vaccination rises and the immunity effect of the whole society grows larger. As a result, such actions of the society reduce the number of diseases and contribute to the effectiveness of the fight against COVID-19.

The highest negative correlation was for the association of social capital with mortality during the pandemic (Figure 2.6).

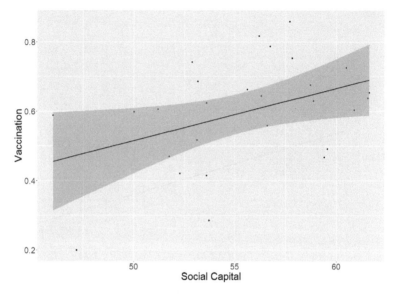

Figure 2.5 Scatterplot of social capital and vaccination (%)
Source: Own study.

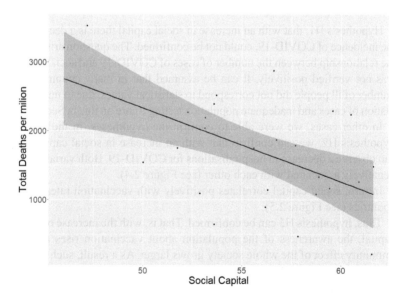

Figure 2.6 Scatterplot of social capital and cumulative total per million population
Source: Own study.

The conducted analysis confirmed hypothesis H4 that a higher proportion of social capital in a country contributes to a reduction in mortality due to COVID-19. It is worth noting that death statistics are what weighs most heavily on the effective management of a pandemic in a country. As of October 31, 2021, the number of confirmed deaths worldwide due to COVID-19 has exceeded 5 million. The pandemic claimed its first million victims within nine months of its announcement; the second – within four months, the third – within three. Another million died in 82 and the fifth one in 112 days. These data show that despite the increasing knowledge of the virus, the effectiveness of the fight against it has not generally increased (*Liczba zgonów na świecie z powodu COVID-19 przekroczyła 5 milionów*, 2021).

As a result of the analysis, it can be concluded that the emergency actions indicated by the governments of EU countries should be respected by the societies as much as possible. The study showed that the attitude of the population to such issues as maintaining social distance, adherence to norms can reduce the impact of the pandemic. In fact, this approach helps to protect people with comorbidities and the elderly, who have been most affected by the pandemic. Thus, the most important things seem to be making the public aware and teaching social responsibility.

In addition to the theoretical value of the present research, which is the verification of the model of the dependence of social capital on the reduction of the effects of COVID-19, it is possible to point out its practical implications. They concern, first of all, the way of organising state activities during the pandemic, including attention to the issue of educating the public of the principles and norms of social coexistence, as well as shared responsibility for the health and life of individuals.

2.3 The role of social and individual capital in crisis management in EU countries during a pandemic

Traditionally, social capital is associated with sociological studies. Increasingly, there are also studies related to the impact of social capital on well-being, economic development, and even innovation (Narayan, 2002, pp. 58–81; Tomala, 2017, pp. 75–90). However, there exist no studies indicating what will happen to social capital during the crisis.

It should be noted that the fight against the COVID-19 virus can be considered a crisis situation that authorities and societies of countries around the world had to face. In the literature on the subject, the crisis is defined in various ways. The essence of the crisis is the uncertainty associated with the lack of designated, proven methods of action. The crisis means a turning point, a decisive moment, or even a turning point. It is connected with such actions as: choosing, deciding, struggling, and fighting, in which it is necessary to act under time pressure. This definition of crisis stems from the original meaning of the word *krisis* (from Greek), which in medicine meant a moment of solstice followed by (or not) a moment of recovery (Morawski, 2003, p. 9). In this part of the study, an attempt was made to answer the question regarding the role of human capital and social capital in combating COVID-19.

2.3.1   *Individual capital versus social capital during the COVID-19 pandemic*

The traditional sociological approach allowed for the examination of rules and principles regarding the functioning of individuals or society. However, there is a lack of consensus in the literature regarding the definition of social capital, which makes it difficult to define it and use quantitative methods to analyse it. In order to better understand what social capital is, it is worth comparing it to human capital because although the terms may seem similar, their meaning is different (Coleman, 2003, p. 57).

The primary difference between human capital and social capital is the effectiveness of the individual and group work and is indicative of whether we can describe a society as the learning entity (Schuller & Field, 1998, pp. 226–235). This may be important in the case of pandemic control. According to Janusz Czapiński, the essence of social capital is team competitiveness based on mutual relations of group members, while the essence of human capital is individual competitiveness based on intellectual, motivational, and symbolic resources (Czapiński, 2008, pp. 5–6). The basic differences between human capital and social capital are shown in Figure 2.7.

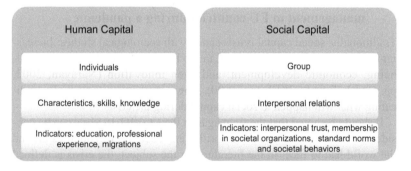

Figure 2.7 Differences between human capital and social capital

Source: Own study based on the data from Czapiński (2008, pp. 5–6).

In the following figure, the limitations of the group of countries of the European Union were adopted, including the UK, which left the EU during the pandemic. The following figure compares intellectual capital and social capital in 28 EU countries (see Figure 2.8):

As the chart indicates, the advantage of social capital over intellectual capital is recorded by such countries as Estonia, Latvia, Luxembourg, Croatia, Ireland, Austria, Slovenia, Lithuania, Portugal, Romania, Belgium, Spain, Italy, Malta, Greece, and Cyprus. Other countries are dominated by intellectual capital, including: Sweden, Denmark, Finland, the United Kingdom, France, the Czech Republic, Slovakia, Germany, Hungary, the Netherlands, Poland, and Bulgaria. Intellectual capital can help increase knowledge about coronavirus, advance research to combat it, and provide better health care during a pandemic. Conversely, in countries where social capital is prevalent, the public will better conform to the norms and regulations imposed by the state's restrictions. This may contribute to limiting the spread of the virus and reducing mortality. The role of vaccination should also be emphasised. It is society and those individuals who understand the importance and significance of this form of prevention that protect not only themselves but also those who are most at risk of complications resulting from the disease.

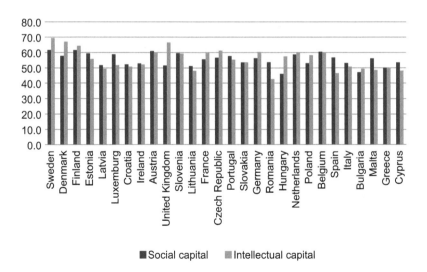

Figure 2.8 Comparison of social and intellectual capital in EU = 28 countries in 2020
Source: Own study based on the data from *Social Capital Index* (2020).

2.3.2   Individual capital and social capital in the fight against COVID-19 in EU countries

To show the role and importance of individual capital in combating COVID-19, Table 2.2 presents the financial outlays and human resources that have been used to fight the pandemic in EU countries. The data were obtained from the reports of individual countries, sent during the period of the pandemic to the European Observatory on Health System and Policies.

Analysing the table, it can be seen that almost all countries have made efforts to mobilise additional medical professionals, retired workers, or students from medical, military, or fire departments. Another form of mobilisation of individual capital has been the efforts of state governments to pay raises, psychological support, or provide child care for those working in the health sector. In addition, individual capital was strengthened through additional financing. The simplest form that EU member states used was the additional funding that governments arranged for the purchase of additional medical equipment, protective gear, tests, etc. Governments in most countries also arranged additional remuneration for medical staff, while companies were less frequently supported. Countries such as Ireland, Sweden, and Poland used the most measures, while Croatia and Romania used the least. In their reports, representatives of less affluent countries, such as Romania, Bulgaria, and others, indicated disproportions in human resources, including the availability of doctors and nurses. It is worth noting that as far as possible most countries have tried to make up for these shortages by hiring additional medical staff and introducing various facilitations, including a faster path to obtaining the right to practise, or retraining courses.

These measures undoubtedly contributed to reducing the impact of the epidemic in the countries studied. However, there is also the issue of social relations, which can weaken or strengthen preventive measures taken by governments or medical experts. Social capital will therefore refer to the interactions between individuals that form groups (Coleman, 1990, p. 302). The concept of social capital was popularised by American researchers R. D. Putman and F. Fukuyama. Francis Fukuyama defined social capital as an attribute only of stable communities, in which there is a permanent and stable political and legal system. According to him, social capital is a set of informal values and ethical norms shared by members of a particular group and enabling them to interact effectively, thus allowing them to act more efficiently. It refers to such values as trust, truthfulness, fulfilment of duties, and reciprocity in relations with others. The main benefit of high social capital is the reduction of transaction costs, i.e. among other things, costs associated with contracting, litigation, and other formal activities. This applies to the economic sphere of life (Fukuyama, 1995, pp. 89–103, 2002,

Table 2.2 Use of human resources and financial capital by EU countries during a pandemic

Country	Utilisation of human resources related to pandemic control								Financing of services related to pandemic control						Total
	Students	Retired doctors	Obtaining license to practise	Military	Psychological support	Professional development courses	Support from NGOs	Providing childcare	Additional finance	Public funds	State or local government funds	Special fund	Assistance to providers losing income	Additional remuneration for health care workers	
Sweden	+				+	+	+	+	+	+	+		+	+	5+5
Denmark	+				+	+					+	+			3+2
Finland	+		+			+			+	+	+			+	3+5
Estonia	+			+	+				+	+				+	3+3
Latvia	+				+				+		+			+	2+3
Luxembourg	+	+				+			+				+		3+2
Croatia					+	+			+	+					2+2
Ireland	+	+	+	+	+	+	+	+	+				+	+	8+3
Austria	+	+	+	+					+	+			+		4+3
United Kingdom	+	+	+	+						+					4+1
Slovenia	+				+				+		+		+		2+3
Lithuania	+	+			+	+		+	+		+			+	5+3
France					+	+		+	+					+	3+2
Czech Republic	+		+			+	+	+	+			+	+		5+3
Portugal		+				+	+	+	+						4+1
Slovakia			+		+				+		+		+	+	2+4
Germany		+	+		+	+		+	+		+			+	5+3
Romania	+			+	+				+						3+1
Hungary	+			+	+		+				+	+			4+2
Netherlands					+		+	+		+	+			+	3+3
Poland	+		+	+				+	+	+	+		+	+	4+5
Belgium	+				+		+			+		+		+	3+3
Spain	+	+			+	+			+		+				4+2
Italy	+	+		+		+			+					+	4+2
Bulgaria	+	+			+				+		+		+	+	3+4
Malta	+			+	+	+		+	+					+	5+2
Greece	+	+			+	+			+		+			+	4+3
Cyprus					+	+			+				+	+	2+3
Total	**21**	**11**	**8**	**9**	**20**	**16**	**7**	**10**	**23**	**9**	**14**	**4**	**11**	**17**	

Source: Own study based on the data from *HSRM Countries* (2021).

pp. 23–37). In other areas, a high level of social capital, according to Fukuyama, is linked to the functioning of a healthy civil state and the formation of groups and associations that are the filler between the state and the family. The lack of social capital creates social dysfunctions (corruption, terrorism, etc.) and can lead to a lack of or lower economic development (Fukuyama, 2000, pp. 3–9). Defined in this way, social capital can be related to adherence to new norms during a pandemic, trust in community organisations, including health experts, presenting information on prevention regarding the spread of COVID-19.

Social capital improves the results of the actions, and it serves as a determinant of social norms and facilitates the flow of information, becomes a guidepost of actions for society, and allows to influence other people (Lounsbury et al., 2002). These characteristics can be applied to pandemic situations. Efficient flow of information during a crisis can be crucial for the public to be easily informed about legal changes, new regulations, restrictions, or support for particular groups such as medical professionals or entrepreneurs. In this context, common values and social norms, which influence the proper distribution of material aid, counteract corruption or mismanagement during a pandemic, etc., will be extremely important. Their proper functioning should ensure better management during a pandemic. The chart below presents data on the attitudes of EU citizens towards democratic principles and values during COVID-19. The analysis is based on the results of the third round of a survey conducted by the European Parliament during COVID-19 in early October 2020. Within, the survey respondents answered the question: Should the EU only provide funds to Member States conditional upon their government's implementation of the rule of law and of democratic principles? Figure 2.9 shows EU citizens' attitudes towards making financial support for the fight against COVID-19 conditional on adherence to common norms and values, particularly adherence to the rule of law and respect for democracy.

As the chart shows, the majority of EU citizens consider important and agree that aid for reconstruction after a pandemic should be allocated on the basis of meeting the criterion of the rule of law and democracy. Czechs were the fewest to agree with this statement – only 58% of respondents, but it is worth noting that this figure represents more than half of the respondents in this country. On average as many as 77% of Europeans insist that EU funds should be linked to respect for the rule of law. This means that almost eight out of ten respondents across the EU support the idea that the EU should only provide funds to Member States if the national government implements the rule of law and democratic principles. Even citizens in countries where the EU has doubts about the rule of law, such as Poland and Hungary, say they want this. The importance of European and community values is

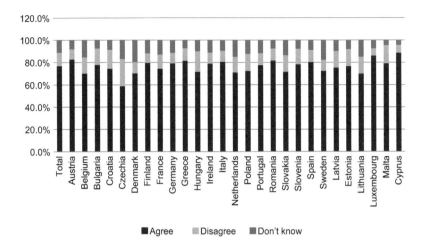

Figure 2.9 EU citizens' attitudes towards making financial support for the fight against COVID-19 conditional on adherence to the rule of law and respect for democracy

Source: Own study based on the data from: *Public opinion in the EU in time of coronavirus crisis 3* (2020).

evidenced by the fact that EU members perceive the EU as an organisation that should have more competence to deal with crises, which is why they demand a larger budget to deal with COVID-19 (European Parliament, 2020). The indication that the EU should become more involved in the fight against the pandemic shows the trust in this organisation and the identification of its citizens with the values that it indicates as the most important.

Fukuyama in his work *Social Capital and Civil Society* mentions effective cooperation, which is the basis for the presence of social capital in a country (Fukuyama, 2000). This aspect is also important to fight the pandemic because of the rapid spread of the virus and the need to conduct special restrictions to limit its transmission. Experts from WHO recommend: "Stay safe by taking some simple precautions, such as physical distancing, wearing a mask, especially when distancing cannot be maintained, keeping rooms well ventilated, avoiding crowds and close contact, regularly cleaning your hands, and coughing into a bent elbow or tissue. Check local advice where you live and work. Do it all!" (WHO, 2020). They argue that by following the new rules of social coexistence, people not only take care of their own health but above all of the health of those whose contact with the virus may prove to be dangerous to health and lead to death due to coexisting diseases. Therefore, it should be emphasised that the responsibility of

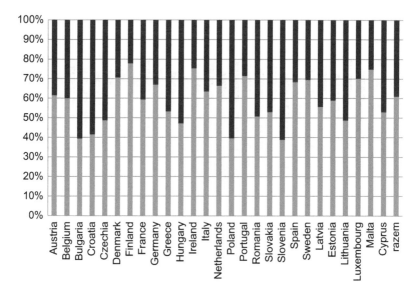

Figure 2.10 Comparison between individual freedom and collective responsibility in the EU

Source: Own study based on the data from *Public opinion in the EU in time of coronavirus crisis 3* (2020).

scientists, physicians, and governments should be to inform and convince people about the effective cooperation of the population in the fight against COVID-19. Figure 2.10 shows the attitude of EU citizens to the willingness to respect restrictions related to COVID-19 and the need for individual freedom in this regard.

As can be seen in the graph, the majority of citizens of European Union countries believe that the fight against COVID-19 justifies the introduction of restrictions and limitation of freedom. The leaders who understand this need and feel a shared responsibility for the health and lives of others are the Finns, the Maltese, and the Irish who by over 70% confirmed the need for and understanding of the introduction of sanitary restrictions in connection with the pandemic. Among the countries where more than half of the respondents consider it important to respect restrictions are Austria,

Belgium, Denmark, France, Germany, Greece, Italy, the Netherlands, Portugal, Slovakia, Spain, Sweden, Latvia, Estonia, Luxembourg, and Cyprus. On average, this represents 58.3% of those surveyed in this group. On the other hand, there is a large group of EU citizens who believe that their freedom is an individual matter and should not be restricted in any way, even in the case of a pandemic. This group includes exclusively countries that only joined the EU in 2004 or later. One can therefore conclude that the new EU members have not assimilated EU values. Hence there is far less shared responsibility and less communitarianism than in the "old EU" countries. Bulgaria, Croatia, the Czech Republic, Hungary, Poland, Romania, Slovenia, and Lithuania belong to the group that does not care about co-responsibility at the time of COVID-19. Therefore, it is worth emphasising that taking care not only of ourselves but also of others is not the strong point of the indicated countries. The question of responsibility concerns not only the European Union as an organisation but also the citizens of the Member States. This shared responsibility is very important because of the EU freedoms, including freedom of movement in the open market. In addition, this responsibility for others primarily relates to our immediate environment, the places and buildings where people live. Understanding this relationship, which is in line with EU values, should be key in countries that are recent members of this organisation. These data show that there is a need to educate new citizens to counteract the pandemic.

Another argument regarding social capital is the ability to influence others. This element plays a very important role because it allows to convince the public about restrictions and limitations without causing opposition or rebellion. Moreover, it allows to convince the public about rules, norms, or needed actions during a pandemic. This was also the case with COVID-19, to convince the public of European countries to perform tests in the early stages of the pandemic, or later, when vaccines were released.

Testing people who may be infected with the SARS-CoV-2 coronavirus is an essential tool for limiting the spread of the epidemic. Because of the continued spread of COVID-19 coronavirus infection, the need to monitor the epidemiological situation in at-risk areas continues. WHO in its recommendations endorses making tests on the basis of clinical and epidemiological indications, taking into account the likelihood of this particular infection. To detect coronavirus causing COVID-19 disease genetic and immunological (serological) tests are used. Performing the tests requires specialised equipment that can be operated by properly trained personnel, as well as adherence to specific safety measures (*COVID-19 Transmission and Protective Measures| WHO Western Pacific*, n.d.).

Lack of shared responsibility for the health and lives of others impacts the number of tests performed for COVID-19. If a country's citizens ignore the danger of COVID-19, they may not be reaching for the simplest and quickest tool to limit the spread of the virus. Another danger of not testing is hiding the true extent of the pandemic because it is those people who have COVID-19 without apparent symptoms that contribute the most to the spread of the virus. Figure 2.11 presents data on the performance of confirmatory testing for the virus.

As the chart shows, there are large disparities in testing citizens for COVID-19 in EU countries. The leaders are Cyprus, Slovakia, Denmark, and Luxembourg, while the worst situation is in Poland. It is worth referring to the messages of experts who emphasise that the serological test can indicate whether the infection has occurred and detect the so-called silent carriers, i.e. people in whom the course of the disease is asymptomatic. Performing tests in a group that already has symptoms of COVID-19 is somewhat unnecessary because it only confirms the diagnosis and does not prevent the spread of the epidemic. Convincing the population to get tested is a very important task for experts and the government. They are responsible for the effectiveness of the fight against COVID-19. Lack of effectiveness in testing is an argument that shows that in countries where the fewest citizens were tested there is no authority among the rulers and medical experts. This is a very important signal that there is a lack of social capital.

Similar to the issue of testing for COVID-19, social credentials can also help convince the public of the need for mass vaccination – as the most important, the only and the most effective way to fight coronavirus. It is important to note that there is a cross-over between two types of capital, i.e. individual capital and social capital. Even if scientists create, produce,

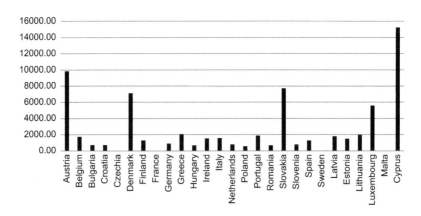

Figure 2.11 Cumulative COVID-19 tests per 1,000 people

Source: Own study based on the data from *COVID-19 Data Explorer* (2021).

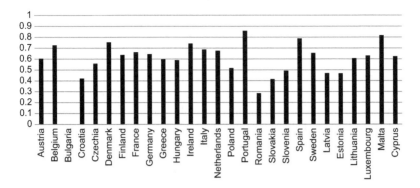

Figure 2.12 Share of people vaccinated against COVID-19
Source: Own study based on the data from Ritchie et al. (2020).

and make available a tool to combat COVID-19 such as a vaccine, the lack of social capital can undermine the achievements of individual capital. Figure 2.12 presents data as of October 5, 2021, on the percentage of vaccinated people in the population in EU countries.

The start of the vaccination process from January 2021 in many parts of the world gave hope that the pandemic would end. As outbreaks continued in the spring of 2021, resulting from the spread of the UK version of the virus, many infectious disease experts called for the population to be vaccinated to combat the pandemic. The main argument raised by the medical profession was that populations acquire group immunity. Community immunity (also known as population immunity, herd immunity, or group immunity) refers to the protection of non-immunised individuals as a result of vaccinating a high percentage of the population. The concept arose from the observation that the presence in a population of persons immunised against a given disease reduces the likelihood that non-immunised persons will also contract that disease. This concept applies to diseases that are transmitted from person to person. The community immunity threshold is defined as the percentage of immunised persons in a population after which the number of new infected persons begins to decline, typically requiring 90%–95% of the population to be immune. However, the percentage of people immunised by vaccination varies from disease to disease.

According to Magdalena Rosińska of the Department of Infectious Disease Epidemiology and Surveillance with the National Institute of Public Health, in the case of SARS-CoV-2 virus, differences in infectivity for individual variants are key. "Ro values for the different variants of SARS-CoV-2:

- Wuhan variant about 3 (one person infects an average of 3 other people, ranging from 2.5 to 3.5 in different populations),
- Alpha variant 4.5 (one person infects 4.5 people),
- Delta variant 7 (one person infects almost 7 people).

Therefore, for the Delta variant we need a population immunisation rate of 86%. If Ro is 7 then the percentage of unvaccinated cannot exceed 1/7=14% (we assume a population immunity threshold at which the epidemic expires r<1 (Ro x <1 a X<1/ Ro)" (Rosińska, 2021).

However, as shown in the graph, in the European Union, only Portugal and Malta come close to achieving group immunity. The countries that come close to meeting the target, i.e. Spain, Denmark, and Ireland, also have satisfactory results in this regard. They are short of achieving group immunity by some 10% of the community. This is a promising result because of the opportunity to vaccinate the youngest citizens who, although they do not get ill or are slightly ill, can transmit the virus. At the opposite end of the spectrum are countries where more than 50% of the population has not been vaccinated. The worst situation is in Romania, where only 28% of people have been vaccinated. In Slovakia and Croatia, where only 42% of the population has chosen to be vaccinated, the situation is also problematic. Slightly higher percentage of vaccinated people, in the range of 46%–48% of the population, was to be found in Estonia, Latvia, and Slovenia. It is here that it can be predicted that the next waves of epidemics will break out. It is in these countries that it will be possible for the virus to mutate and new variants to emerge. It should be emphasised that despite the scientific evidence of the importance and role of vaccination in virus control (medical aspect) the percentage of vaccinated population in many countries is still insufficient.

To sum up the aforementioned considerations, it is worth comparing the amount of social capital presented by individual EU countries to the behaviour of societies resulting from the occurrence of COVID-19. The following table compares the indicators analysed earlier, dividing countries into those whose indicators are higher or lower than the EU average in selected areas.

Summarising the aforementioned discussion, the validity of the arguments regarding the role of social capital in the fight against COVID-19 can be confirmed. An important feature of social capital is the trust and shared values that members of a community possess. Thus, when individuals with similar civic virtues come together and establish relationships, an additional shared quality is created that benefits all members of the community. On the basis of the aforementioned analysis, it can be concluded that there is a significant stock of social capital in the countries of the European Union, which has resulted in positive attitudes to the crisis situation during the

Table 2.3 Comparison of social capital during the pandemic

Państwo	Social capital	Norms and values	Trust	Collective responsibility
Sweden	+	−	+	+
Denmark	+	−	+	+
Finland	+	+	+	+
Estonia	+	+	−	+
Latvia	−	−	−	−
Luxemburg	+	+	+	+
Croatia	−	−	−	−
Ireland	−	+	+	+
Austria	+	+	−	+
Slovenia	+	+	−	−
Lithuania	−	−	−	−
France	+	−	+	+
Czechia	+	−	−	−
Portugal	+	+	+	+
Slovakia	−	−	−	−
Germany	+	+	+	+
Romania	−	+	−	−
Hungary	−	−	−	−
Netherlands	+	−	+	+
Poland	−	−	−	−
Belgium	+	−	+	−
Spain	+	+	+	+
Italy	−	+	+	+
Bulgaria	−	+	NA	−
Malta	+	+	+	+
Greece	−	+	−	−
Cyprus	−	+	+	−

Source: Own study based on the data from *Public opinion in the EU in time of coronavirus crisis 3* (2020), *Social Capital Index* (2020), Ritchie et al. (2020).

pandemic period. The six countries (Finland, Malta, Germany, Spain, Luxembourg, and Portugal) with high levels of social capital affirmed commitment in all of the areas analysed, i.e. the issue of vaccination, responsibility in complying with restrictions, or making financial solidarity conditional on respect for the rule of law and democracy. Conversely, the five countries that showed the lowest social capital among EU states did not confirm responsibility for vaccination issues, restrictions, or EU aid. An interesting case in point are two countries (Ireland and Italy) that, although they have less social capital, showed positive attitudes towards pandemic control in the areas studied. Moreover, the analysis shows that EU citizens are united by common values, among which the most important is the respect for law and democratic values. This is especially true for countries that have been in the EU for a long time and belong to the so-called old EU countries. It is among them that greater shared responsibility can be observed, which results from the recommended actions of both the WHO and medical representatives in Member States. In contrast, less social capital is associated with shorter EU membership and thus less shared responsibility for the spread of COVID-19.

References

About Solability. (2021). https://solability.com/about-solability
Andrzejewski, M. (2010). Wybrane problemy zarządzania kryzysowego w organizacji. *Acta Universitatis Lodziensis. Folia Oeconomica, 234*, 163.
Bland, A. R., Roiser, J. P., Mehta, M. A., Sahakian, B. J., Robbins, T. W., & Elliott, R. (2021). The impact of COVID-19 social isolation on aspects of emotional and social cognition. *Cognition and Emotion*, 1–10. https://doi.org/10.1080/0269993 1.2021.1892593
Borgonovi, F., & Andrieu, E. (2020). Bowling together by bowling alone: Social capital and COVID-19. *Social Science & Medicine, 265*, 113501. https://doi.org/10.1016/j.socscimed.2020.113501
Borgonovi, F., Andrieu, E., & Subramanian, S. V. (2021). The evolution of the association between community level social capital and COVID-19 deaths and hospitalizations in the United States. *Social Science & Medicine, 278*, 113948. https://doi.org/10.1016/j.socscimed.2021.113948
Bourdieu, P. (1986). The forms of capital. In J. Richardson (Ed.), *Handbook of theory and research for the sociology of education* (pp. 15–29). Greenwood.
Bourdieu, P., & Wacquant, J. (2006). Logika pól. In A. Jasińska-Kania (Ed.), *Współczesne teorie socjologiczne. 1 1*. Wydawnictwo Naukowe "Scholar."
Bourguignon, J., & Sprenger, E. (2021). Restoring public trust after Trump and COVID-19. *Intereconomics, 56*(1), 2–3. https://doi.org/10.1007/s10272-021-0941-5
Cairney, P., & Wellstead, A. (2020). COVID-19: Effective policymaking depends on trust in experts, politicians, and the public. *Policy Design and Practice*, 1–14. https://doi.org/10.1080/25741292.2020.1837466
Cappello, G., & Rizzuto, F. (2020). Journalism and fake news in the COVID-19 era. Perspectives for media education in Italy. *Media Education, 11*(2). https://doi.org/10.36253/me-9682
Coleman, J. (1988). Social capital in the creation of human capital. *The American Journal of Sociology, 94*, 95–120. www.jstor.org/stable/2780243.
Coleman, J. (1990). *Foundations of social theory*. Belknap Press of Harvard University Press.
Coleman, J. (2003). Social capital in the creation of human capital. In R. L. Cross, A. Parker, & L. Sasson (Eds.), *Networks in the knowledge economy*. Oxford University Press.

COVID-19 Data Explorer. (2021). *Our world in data*. https://ourworldindata.org/coronavirus-data-explorer

COVID-19 transmission and protective measures| WHO Western Pacific. (n.d.). Retrieved October 19, 2021, from www.who.int/westernpacific/emergencies/COVID-19/information/COVID-19-testing

Czapiński, J. (2008). Kapitał ludzki i kapitał społeczny a dobrobyt materialny. Polski paradoks. *Zarządzanie Publiczne, 2*(4), 4–28.

Data on hospital and ICU admission rates and current occupancy for COVID-19. (2021, October 28). *European centre for disease prevention and control*. www.ecdc.europa.eu/en/publications-data/download-data-hospital-and-icu-admission-rates-and-current-occupancy-COVID-19

Dohle, S., Wingen, T., & Schreiber, M. (2020). Acceptance and adoption of protective measures during the COVID-19 pandemic: The role of trust in politics and trust in science. *Social Psychological Bulletin, 15*(4), e4315. https://doi.org/10.32872/spb.4315

Elgar, F. J., Stefaniak, A., & Wohl, M. J. A. (2020). The trouble with trust: Time-series analysis of social capital, income inequality, and COVID-19 deaths in 84 countries. *Social Science & Medicine, 263*, 113365. https://doi.org/10.1016/j.socscimed.2020.113365

European Commission. (2021). *Social science studies*. www.recover-europe.eu/social-sciences-studies/

European Parliament. (2020, October). *Europeans insist EU funds be linked to respect for rule of law*. www.europarl.europa.eu/at-your-service/pl/be-heard/eurobarometer/public-opinion-in-the-eu-in-time-of-coronavirus-crisis-3

Fukuyama, F. (1995). Social capital and the global economy. *Foreign Affairs, 74*(5), 89. https://doi.org/10.2307/20047302

Fukuyama, F. (2000). Social capital and civil society. *IMF Working Papers, 00*(74), 1. https://doi.org/10.5089/9781451849585.001

Fukuyama, F. (2002). Social capital and development: The coming agenda. *SAIS Review, 22*(1), 23–37. https://doi.org/10.1353/sais.2002.0009

Hartley, K., & Jarvis, D. S. L. (2020). Policymaking in a low-trust state: Legitimacy, state capacity, and responses to COVID-19 in Hong Kong. *Policy and Society, 39*(3), 403–423. https://doi.org/10.1080/14494035.2020.1783791

HSRM Countries. (2021). https://eurohealthobservatory.who.int/monitors/hsrm/hsrm-countries

Laurence, J., & Kim, H. H. (2021). Individual and community social capital, mobility restrictions, and psychological distress during the COVID-19 pandemic: A multilevel analysis of a representative US survey. *Social Science & Medicine*, 114361. https://doi.org/10.1016/j.socscimed.2021.114361

Li, N., Li, S., & Fan, L. (2021). Risk factors of psychological disorders after the COVID-19 outbreak: The mediating role of social support and emotional intelligence. *Journal of Adolescent Health*, S1054139X2100375X. https://doi.org/10.1016/j.jadohealth.2021.07.018

Liczba zgonów na świecie z powodu COVID-19 przekroczyła 5 milionów. (2021, October 5). *Rzeczpospolita*. www.rp.pl/ochrona-zdrowia/art19064011-liczba-zgonow-na-swiecie-z-powodu-COVID-19-przekroczyla-5-milionow

Liu, Q., & Wen, S. (2021). Does social capital contribute to prevention and control of the COVID-19 pandemic? Empirical evidence from China. *International Journal of Disaster Risk Reduction, 64*, 102501. https://doi.org/10.1016/j.ijdrr.2021.102501

Lounsbury, M., Lin, N., Cook, K., & Burt, R. S. (2002). Social capital: Theory and research. *Contemporary Sociology, 31*(1), 28. https://doi.org/10.2307/3089402

Morawski, W. (2003). *Kronika kryzysów gospodarczych*. TRIO.

Narayan, D. (2002). Bonds and bridges: Social capital and economic development. In J. Isham, T. Kelly, & S. Ramaswamy (Eds.), *Well-being in development countries*. Edward Elgar.

Narodowe Centrum Nauki. (2020). *Szybka ścieżka dostępu do funduszy na badania nad Covi-19*. www.gov.pl/web/edukacja-i-nauka/nauka-przeciw-COVID-19

National Institutes of Health. (2021). *COVID-19 research*. https://covid19.nih.gov/

Public opinion in the EU in time of coronavirus crisis 3. (2020). *Public opinion in the EU in time of coronavirus crisis 3*. www.europarl.europa.eu/at-your-service/pl/be-heard/eurobarometer/public-opinion-in-the-eu-in-time-of-coronavirus-crisis-3

Putnam, R. D. (1995). Bowling alone: America's declining social capital. *Journal of Democracy, 6*(1), 65–78. https://doi.org/10.1353/jod.1995.0002

Putnam, R. D. (2001). Social capital. measurement and consequences. *Printemps, Spring*, 41–51.

Ritchie, H., Mathieu, E., Rodés-Guirao, L., Appel, C., Giattino, C., Ortiz-Ospina, E., Hasell, J., Macdonald, B., Beltekian, D., & Roser, M. (2020). Coronavirus pandemic (COVID-19). *Our world in data*. https://ourworldindata.org/covid-vaccinations

Rosińska, M. (2021). *Jak wyliczono próg odporności zbiorowiskowej populacji dla wariantu Delta wirusa SARS-CoV-2?* https://szczepienia.pzh.gov.pl/wszystko-o-szczepieniach/co-to-jest-odpornosc-zbiorowiskowa/

Schuller, T., & Field, J. (1998). Social capital, human capital and the learning society. *International Journal of Lifelong Education, 17*(4), 226–235. https://doi.org/10.1080/0260137980170402

Social Capital Index. (2020). *SOLABILITY*. https://solability.com/the-global-sustainable-competitiveness-index/the-index/social-capital/

Social Capital Index. (2021). *SOLABILITY*. https://solability.com/the-global-sustainable-competitiveness-index/the-index/social-capital

Thanh Le, T., Andreadakis, Z., Kumar, A., Gómez Román, R., Tollefsen, S., Saville, M., & Mayhew, S. (2020). The COVID-19 vaccine development landscape. *Nature Reviews Drug Discovery, 19*(5), 305–306. https://doi.org/10.1038/d41573-020-00073-5

Tittenbrun, J. (2016). Concepts of capital in Pierre Bourdieu's theory. *Miscellanea Anthropologica et Sociologica, 1*(17), 81–103.

Tomala, M. (2017). Social capital in Baltic Sea region in the light of the concept by Pierre Bourdieu. *Miscellanea Oeconomicae, 4*(II), 75–90.

Turner, J. H., Woroniecka, G., & Manterys, A. (2004). *Struktura teorii socjologicznej*. Wydaw. Naukowe PWN.

Watkins, J. (2020). Preventing a COVID-19 pandemic. *BMJ*, m810. https://doi.org/10.1136/bmj.m810

Weissleder, R., Lee, H., Ko, J., & Pittet, M. J. (2020). COVID-19 diagnostics in context. *Science Translational Medicine*, *12*(546), eabc1931. https://doi.org/10.1126/scitranslmed.abc1931

WHO. (2020). *How can we protect others and ourselves if we don't know who is infected?* www.who.int/news-room/q-a-detail/coronavirus-disease-COVID-19

WHO. (2021a). *COVID-19 vaccine tracker and landscape.* www.who.int/publications/m/item/draft-landscape-of-COVID-19-candidate-vaccines

WHO. (2021b). *Global research on coronavirus disease (COVID-19).* www.who.int/emergencies/diseases/novel-coronavirus-2019/global-research-on-novel-coronavirus-2019-ncov

3 Can the European economy survive the coronavirus crisis?

Aleksandra Kordonska

Introduction

Outbreaks of diseases (such as cholera, bubonic plague, smallpox, and influenza) across international borders are defined as pandemic, killing millions of people. Throughout history, disease outbreaks have ravaged humanity, affecting it and sometimes changing the trajectory of history. As humans have spread across the world, so have infectious diseases. Widespread trade created opportunities for human and animal interactions. The more civilised humans have become – with larger cities, more exotic trade routes, and increased contact with different populations of people, animals, and ecosystems – the more likely pandemics would occur. Even in this modern era, outbreaks are nearly constant, though not every outbreak reaches pandemic level as the coronavirus has.

Despite the fact that the virus which emerged in Wuhan (China) has quickly spread all around the world, which is globalised and interconnected as never before, every country responds to pandemic on its own, while the decisions, made by the governments, directly affect people's lives. The main goal of Chapter 3 is to assess the influence of the pandemic crisis on the economy of EU states and to define whether the European economy can survive the crisis. This chapter aims to address the following key questions:

1 What is the impact of COVID-19 on the EU economy and how is the impact distributed among different sectors?
2 How comprehensive are the recovery measures and to what extent are they meeting the needs of the EU?
3 Whether the economic support has been provided in accordance with changes in the level of restrictions?
4 What is the proper policy response to problematic long-term economic trends?

DOI: 10.4324/9781003222538-3

The first part of the chapter contains an overall analysis of the economic effects of COVID-19 in EU countries based on main economic indicators. The second part reveals the impact of COVID-19 on EU industries. The next part highlights the assessment of the EU response to the coronavirus by using Pearson correlation to define the relationship between the level of restrictions, economic support, and confidence in economy of the EU citizens in selected states. The last part presents a long-term perspective of the pandemic in the EU countries as well as the key recommendations on the recovery measures and policies.

3.1 Economic effects of COVID-19 in EU countries

The COVID-19 pandemic has raised a range of challenges for the EU and deepened existing weaknesses. The EU economy has suffered in 2020 a large recession in common with territorial inequalities across countries and regions. Stricter measures and lockdowns have contributed to high output swathes of economic activity. A decrease in output was caused by a decline in private consumption due to restricted access to certain goods and services and also by the rise in precautionary savings.

According to the Atlantic Council (2020), it could be found three major economic similarities between the COVID-19 and 2008 crisis. First of all, both crises share uncertainty (i.e. non-quantifiable risk) in two leading economies (the United States in 2008 and China in the end of 2019) and spread globally. The second one concerns the initial drops in the stock exchanges of major countries (up to one-fourth of their valuation) have been analogous between both crises. And both global recessions have been successively qualified as the largest since the Great Depression (see: Bordo & Sinha, 2016). And the last one – to limit such shocks, monetary and fiscal policies have in both cases provided massive support.

Considering main economic measures, Figure 3.1 shows gross domestic product and value added for the EU (EU-27) between 2000 and 2020 (market prices, million euro), as well as the main GDP aggregates such as final consumption expenditure, expenditure of government, investment (gross fixed capital formation), and exports and imports of goods and services.

The data reflect obvious decline in all aggregates caused by Covid-19 in 2020 (see: Eurostat, 2021b; OECD 2020a; OECD, 2021b; OECD, 2021d). So, the impact on the economy of EU has been even hardest than due to the global financial crisis (see, e.g. OECD, 2020b). According to the survey of Eurostat (2020a), gross value added decreased by 3.2%, while the real GDP by 6.1%. In particular, household consumption expenditure declined by 4.2% in the EU [i.e. Italy (−6.6%), Belgium and Spain (both −6.5%)]. The only positive growths rates were observed for Hungary (+1.0%) and Slovakia (+0.2%). General government consumption fell by 0.6% [the strongest decline and

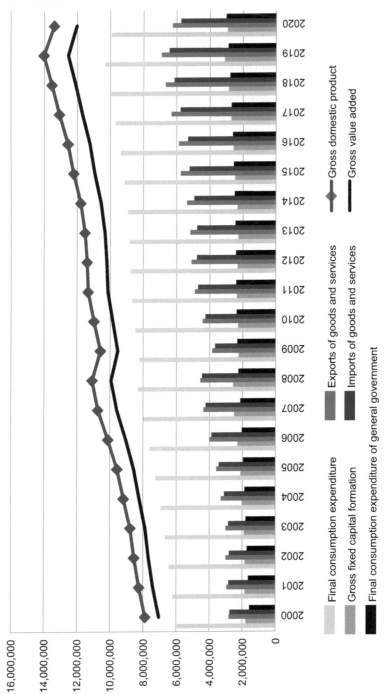

Figure 3.1 Gross domestic product, value added for the EU (EU-27) and the main GDP aggregates (market prices, million euro)

Source: Authors' elaboration, based on data from Eurostat.

increase was recorded in Romania (−12.5%) and Slovenia (+8.9%) respectively]. For the other main expenditure items, gross-fixed capital formation [dropped by 1.8%, i.e. Malta (−21.9%), Luxembourg (−18.4%), Ireland (+32.2%), Cyprus (+15.1%)], exports [fell by 3.4%, i.e. Finland (−8.6%)] and imports [fell by 3.1%, i.e. Spain (−6.6%)], significant decreases were observed in most countries. Positive growth rates were only observed in a few countries, such as Sweden (+3.4% for exports) and Greece (+5.4% for imports).

In the EU, the government debt-to-GDP ratio increased from 77.2% at the end of 2019 to 90.1% at the end of 2020. Thirteen Member States had government debt ratios higher than 60% of GDP, with the highest registered in Greece (206.3%), Italy (155.6%), Portugal (135.2%), Spain (120.0%), Cyprus (115.3%), France (115.0%), and Belgium (112.8%) (Eurostat, 2021g). Deficits and debt ratios have soared in all Member States, with the EU headline deficit increasing to about 7% of GDP in 2020 from 0.5% of GDP in 2019 (Eurostat, 2021g). The largest decrease was noted in Greece [−1.2 percentage points (p.p.)], Malta (−10.2 p.p.), Austria (−8.9 p.p.), Spain and Slovenia (both −8.1 p.p.), while the lowest − in Sweden (−3.4 p.p.), Latvia (−3.9 p.p.), Slovakia and Denmark (both −4.2 p.p.), Finland (−4.5 p.p.), and Romania (−4.9 p.p.) (Eurostat, 2021g).

Considering the contribution of each sector to the annual growth of nominal gross value added (GVA) in euro area at basic prices (which is equal to GDP at market prices minus taxes plus subsidies on products) (Figure 3.2), the gross value added of non-financial corporations delivers the largest contribution to GDP growth but is quite volatile with a large decrease in 2020. The contribution of value added generated in the household sector fluctuates less, partly because of the stabilising influence of the imputed rent on owner-occupied dwellings. The contributions of the financial corporations and government sectors are rather small. The non-financial corporations' sector includes all private and public entities with independent legal status (and close substitutes) that produce goods and non-financial services to the market (Eurostat, 2021a). These data also show that compared to 2009, the impact on the economy has been harder than due to the global financial crisis.

Figure 3.3 presents household gross disposable income and household spending as the amount of individual final consumption expenditure made by resident households to meet their everyday needs, household gross saving and investment rates and gross fixed capital formation. In the second quarter of 2020, the household saving rate (neither seasonally adjusted nor calendar adjusted data) was 26.76 p.p. (compared with 14.42 p.p. in the previous quarter); individual final consumption − (−9.82%), gross disposable income of households − (−2.44%), while gross fixed capital formation − (−17.6%).

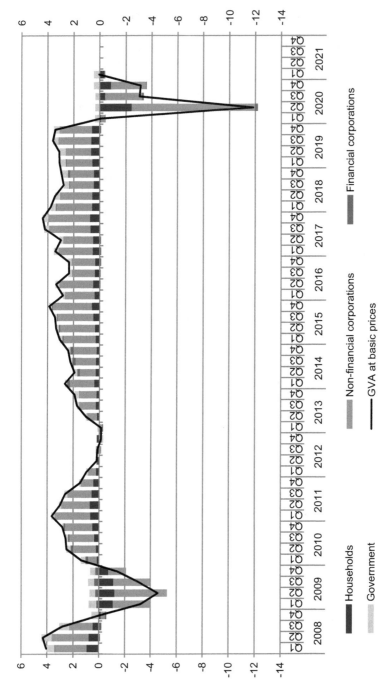

Figure 3.2 Contributions of sectors to the growth of nominal gross value added in the euro area (annual percentage change and percentage point contributions)

Source: Authors' elaboration, based on data from Eurostat and ECB.

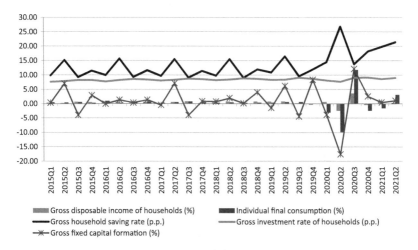

Figure 3.3 Change of capital formation, household saving rate, investment rate, individual final consumption, and disposable income of households in the EU-27 (quarterly, based on non-seasonally adjusted data)

Source: Authors' elaboration, based on Eurostat.

Thus, the household saving rate at EU continued with large increase (the highest is observed in Slovenia (+20.8 p.p.), followed by Ireland (+12.8 p.p.) mainly due to a large decrease in household individual consumption expenditure [i.e. Slovenia (−15.4%), Spain (−11.2%)] (Eurostat, 2021d). Denmark was the only country where household saving rate decreased (by −2.7 p.p.) while household consumption increased (by 0.2%) (Eurostat, 2021d). In general, the only sharp change from 2019 was in the third quarter of 2020, when the saving rate fell to 13.75 p.p. and the consumption grew to 11.75%. During 2020, the household investment rate increased slightly to 9.08 p.p. in fourth quarter, compared to 7.63 p.p. in the second quarter. Household disposable income in the UE was quite volatile in 2020 (−2.44% – in the second quarter, 3.58% – in the third quarter, and (−0.45%) – in the fourth quarter). As in the two previous quarters, the contributions to that growth (both the positive and negative ones) were very different to the 2011–2020 period. Social benefits (other than social transfers in kind) provided the largest positive contribution, while property income was the largest negative contributor. The main contributor to the decrease in Spain and Italy was compensation of employees, while in Denmark, it was other current transfers, taxes on income, wealth, etc. (Eurostat, 2021d).

3.2   Impact of COVID-19 on EU industries

Considering sectoral impacts, services have been most affected. The cultural and creative industries (based on human contact and interactions), the aerospace sector, automotive, textile, food, and health sectors have been suffering more than others. At the beginning of 2020 manufacturing and construction experienced a larger hit, but at the end of the year, we can observe the return to pre-pandemic levels of production. Manufacturing industries have been impacted by short-term supply shortages due to closed factories and borders in the UE as well as beyond. The first wave of pandemic led to decrease in employment, drop in demand and production losses in almost all manufacturing industries; disruptions in global supply chains due to closure of factories in Europe and China; additional costs due to intensified health and security measures (Table 3.1). Nevertheless, most manufacturing-based industries have slowly recovered during the third quarter of 2020 (Table 3.1). Thus, the second wave seems to have been less harmful than the first one because borders and factories remained open, while workplaces had adapted to requirements and realities of the pandemic. Meanwhile, it is worth noting that the pandemic has a harmful impact on small- and medium-sized enterprises.

In comparison with the global financial crisis, the COVID-19 hit the industries in a much more severe way. Within one year (from April 2008 to April 2009), industrial production was reduced by more than 22 index points. Meanwhile, between February and April 2020, the index for total industrial production dropped by almost 29 points (Eurostat, 2021c).

3.3   Assessment of EU response to the coronavirus: Restrictions, economic support, and confidence in economy of EU citizens

This part of Chapter 3 aims to address the following questions:

1   Whether the economic support has been provided in accordance with changes in the level of restrictions?
2   To what extent a confidence in economy of EU citizens depends on the level of restrictions?
3   To what extent a confidence in economy of EU citizens depends on economic support such as income support, debt relief for households, fiscal measures, and support to other countries?

Our study is based on the data from Eurostat and Oxford Coronavirus Government Response Tracker project, i.e.: Stringency Index, Economic Support Index, Economic Sentiment, and Confidence Indicators. To show

Table 3.1 Impact of COVID-19 on EU industries

Industry	The role in the economy	First wave	Second wave
Automotive industries	• Value added: 5% of the EU Total value added; • Employment: 2.6 million people; • 8.5% of all EU manufacturing jobs	• Production losses: 22.3% of the EU total production in 2020; • Demand for cars decreased by 28.3% compared to the 2019; • Supply chains were disrupted due to closure of factories in Europe and China; • 1.1 million jobs were affected directly; many were re-employed on short-term contracts The COVID-19 pandemic accelerates the growth of the electric vehicle market (also due to recovery measures linked to the green transition). The average share of electric car sales over total car sales increased from 3.4% in 2019 to 7.8% in the first half of 2020. Electrified vehicles increased their market share to 26.8%.	• Less severe in the stringency of measures; • Substantially higher car purchasing incentives, including tax incentives and purchase subsidies from governments; • Registration offices and service centres have remained open during the lockdowns; • The EU car market contracted by 23.7% compared to 2019 (about 9.9 million units in 2020)
Aerospace industries (including military aviation)	• Total turnover: EUR 260 billion; • Employment: 890,000 direct jobs; • A "strategic ecosystem," (increasing supply capacity within the EU Single Market)	• A drop in demand for civil aviation (86.1% decline in air traffic in March 2020 and 92.8% in mid-April compared to 2019 levels); • A drop in the demand for the production of aircrafts, disruptions in the supply of raw materials caused by the limitations in cross-border movements; supply delays, massive fallouts in production	• About 191,000 direct jobs were lost for the whole European industry; • A traffic decrease at a weekly daily average of −73% between September and December; • European demand for aerospace manufacturing decreased in overall by 43% in 2020; • Net losses of airlines, airports, and air navigation service providers, national markets in the EU were between 40% and 73% as compared to 2019; • Flights decreases ranging from 61% in the United Kingdom to 56% in Germany and 60% in Italy

(Continued)

Table 3.1 (Continued)

Industry	The role in the economy	First wave	Second wave
Chemical industry	• Turnover: EUR 7,320 billion; • Employment: 12% of EU manufacturing; • Europe is the second largest chemicals producer (16.9% of the total global sales)	• Disruptions in global supply chains, drops in consumption, and manufacturing; • Fall in demand resulted in shrinking production and reduced supply; • Output dropped by 5.2% compared to the previous year's levels (January–June 2020) • The output of medical industry (for instance, of disinfectants) experienced growth following increasing demand	• Q3 experienced an increase of 6.1% from the previous quarter; • The total output dropped by 2.8% from January to November 2020 compared to 2019
Construction industries	• Employment: 18 million direct jobs within the EU; • about 9% contribution to the EU's GDP in 2019 (EUR 1,216 billion)	• Labour shortages, supply chain disruptions, shortages of construction material; additional costs due to intensified health and security measures; • Reduction of capacity (25%–30%); • The winter slowdown in production −20%; until August 2020, production recovered from −11.5% year-on-year growth to −9.1%; • Temporary lay-offs and reduced hours	• less affected; • production recovering almost to the pre-crisis level (97.5%, November 2020); • no shortages of inputs
Food & drink industries	• Employment: 4.82 million people; • Value added: EUR 266 billion (2019)	• Much lower decline in production compared to total manufacturing production (−9.1% in Q2 2019); • Supply chains fluctuations; • Hotellerie-Restaurant-Café (HORECA) was hit the hardest; • Packaged food sales in Germany increased by 56% during late March (compared to 2019); • Sales of frozen foods have been 63% higher in France (compared to 2019);	• (HORECA) negatively affected but less intense; • no shortages; • supply chains remained resilient; • production (with an 8.2% increase) and turnover (with 5.9% increase) recover in Q3 2020 compared to Q2; • decrease in employment: 1.2% for food and 2.2% for drinks industries

Textiles & apparel industries	• About 170,000 companies (99.8% of which are micro-companies and SMEs); • Yearly turnover: EUR 180 billion, • Employment: 1.7 million people	• Shutdown of shops, drop in demand for clothing subsector; • Retail sales falling by 18.8% during Q1; • A drop in production (10% in Q1) and considerable disruption in textile supply chains, creating spill-overs at the cross-regional level; • Employment: a 1.5% decrease in textile and 4.9% in clothing (thanks to the short-term measures taken at the national level to support employment); • Fashion enterprises shifted part of their production to new categories of products; • Imports for traditional textile items from China decreased; • Imports for masks from China increased from EUR 0.5 billion to EUR 12 billion from 2019 to 2020	• Slow recovering in Q3 2020; • Increase in sales through online channels; • Change in consumer behaviour towards e-commerce; • A rebound of production from Q2 by 25% in the textiles and 33% in the clothing subsectors; • Overall retail sales recovery by 62% from Q2; • All-year trend: a drop in production and retail sales for clothing (15% and 9.4%) and textile (7% and 9.7%)
Cultural & creative industries	• Turnover: EUR 643 billion; • 4.4% of the EU GDP; • Employment: 7.6 million people (4% of total employment)	• Almost all cultural production sites were forced to close; • A drop in sales over to 30% during the first two months of the crisis; • Adaptation of some business models to new circumstances (e.g. online performances, virtual museum visits); • New value chains in the music, cinema and publishing industries; • A solid uptake in television, streaming, music, and radio services; • Large profits: technology and logistics providers and suppliers of home-based leisure (e.g. Netflix, Amazon, Facebook); • The emergence of new activities, including home-based arts and crafts, and practitioners	• Certain production activities re-started, and cultural production places partly re-opened (in summer); • Shutdown of spaces that had benefitted from partial re-opening (in autumn); • A net decrease in revenues by 31% in 2020 (worth EUR 199 billion); • Acceleration of digital trends doesn't compensate the losses; • Revenue decrease: music (90%) and performing arts (76%)

(Continued)

Table 3.1 (Continued)

Industry	The role in the economy	First wave	Second wave
Digital industries	• Employment: more than 6 million people; • 4.77% of the EU27 value-added (EUR 645 billion)	• The penetration of Information and Communications Technology (ICT) and digital adoption; • Disruption in supply chains; a drop in production; • Fall in demand hit the manufacturing part of the sector's supply chains; • Increased demand for digital infrastructure; • Total employment increased by 0.5% in Q2 compared to the previous year, hours worked per person decreased by 6.4% in the same period; • Annual change in value-added: a decrease of 4.8% (the smallest drop among sectors)	• In general not affected by pandemic (SMEs have been hit particularly hard); • Growth in demand by 4.6% for devices and by 4% for the software market; • Employment: grew by 0.9% in Q3; • The value-added: increased by 1.8% in Q3
Healthcare industries	• Employment: more than 7 million jobs in 2018; • The pharmaceutical industry is a key industry within the EU economy (EUR 213 billion in market value); • Medical technology sector (EUR 120 billion in 2018; about 730,000 jobs)	• Income of hospitals decreased (more profitable surgeries and check-ups have been cancelled); • Dropped demand for treatments and equipment, in particular, the generic pharmaceuticals sector; • Inconsistencies in the demand-supply ratio; • A drop in pharma retail trade by about 12% in April; • Supply chain challenges (closed factories and borders); • Shortages of pharmaceuticals and healthcare equipment; • Confinement of workers as well as stockpiling of medical masks	• Shortages prevented; • Increase in production in the innovative pharmaceutical sector; • Retail in pharmaceuticals has increased by 12% (September 2020); • Recover of the sector by 98% to pre-crisis level

Source: Authors' elaboration based on data from Eurostat, OECD, IMF, and De Vet et al. (2021) Some differences could be observed among sectors in the level of impact (Figure 3.4). Thus, pharmaceutical production and production of computers and other devices have been affected the least. In 2021, these industries reached almost 146% and 123%, respectively, of the 2015 level. Other manufacturing industries have been hit relatively hard during the first wave and undertook a path towards recovery during the second wave of pandemic (Figure 3.4).

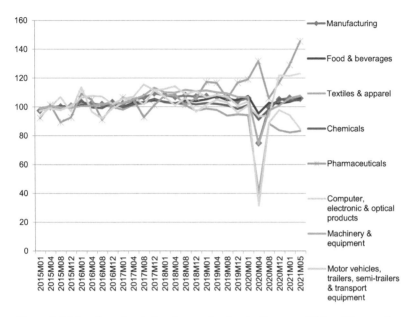

Figure 3.4 Manufacturing industries production in European Union-27 countries (Volume index, 2015 = 100)

Source: Authors' elaboration, based on Eurostat.

the relationship between variables, we estimated a Pearson correlation coefficient.

Ritchie et al. (2020) developed a Stringency Index within the Oxford Coronavirus Government Response Tracker project. The data are collected from publicly available information by a cross-disciplinary Oxford University team led by the Blavatnik School of Government. The index records the strictness of "lockdown style" policies and is a composite measure of nine of the response metrics: school closures, workplace closures, cancellation of public events, restrictions on public gatherings, closures of public transport, stay-at-home requirements, public information campaigns, restrictions on internal movements, and international travel controls (Ritchie et al., 2020). A higher score indicates a stricter response (i.e. 100 = strictest response) of government policies.

Economic Support Index records measures such as income support, debt relief for households, fiscal measures (monetary value USD of fiscal stimuli, including spending or tax cuts), and providing support to other countries (Ritchie et al., 2020). Debt or contract relief captures if the government is freezing financial obligations during the COVID-19 pandemic, such as stopping loan repayments, preventing services like water from stopping, or banning evictions. Income support captures if the government is covering the salaries or providing direct cash payments, universal basic income, or similar, of people who lose their jobs or cannot work.

Using daily data from March 2020 to October 2021, an simple arithmetic average is calculated to assess the level of restrictions in the EU states and the level of economic support (Figure 3.5). Thus, considering the strictness of "lockdown style," policies we can confirm the results obtained in Chapter 1 about quite similar level of restrictions in EU states (Figure 3.5). In terms of the Economic Support Index, the highest level is observed in Cyprus (100), Ireland (98.42), the United Kingdom (96.05), Austria (94.45), and Slovak Republic (91.24), while the lowest in Germany (41.28), Sweden (48.98), Hungary (49.94), Croatia (55.67), France (58.02), and Estonia (59.71) (Figure 3.5).

The dependence between Stringency Index and Economic Support Index in the EU countries based on Pearson correlation makes it possible to define whether the economic support has been provided in accordance with changes in the level of restrictions (Figure 3.6). In some countries, such as Cyprus or the United Kingdom, where the Economic Support Index was

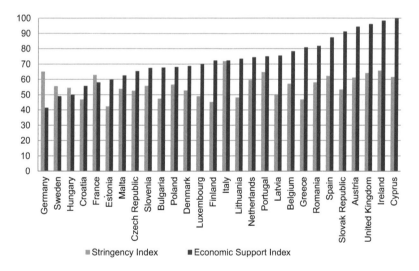

Figure 3.5 Stringency Index (100 = strictest response) and Economic Support Index
           in EU-27 countries from March 2020 to October 2021 (arithmetic average)

Source: Authors' calculations, based on daily data retrieved from https://data.humdata.org/
event/covid-19.

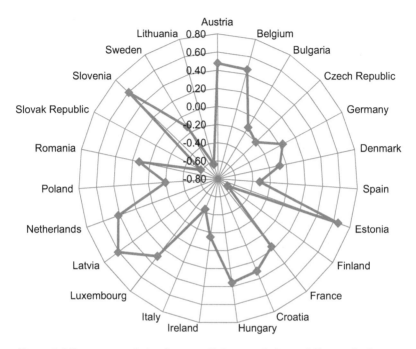

Figure 3.6 Pearson correlation between Stringency Index and Economic Support
Index from April 2020 to October 2021 in EU countries

Source: Authors' calculations, based on daily data retrieved from https://data.humdata.org/
event/covid-19.

100% during the period of observation, it is not possible to estimate the correlation. Meanwhile, the positive correlation is revealed in such countries
as: Austria (0.48), Belgium (0.45), Estonia (0.66), Croatia (0.31), Hungary
(0.36), Luxemburg (0.31), Latvia (0.61), the Netherlands (0.42), Romania
(0.12), and Slovenia (0.59). Thus, we can state that in these states, a stricter
response of government policies has gone in line with the growing level of
economic support. Meanwhile, in some countries, we can observe a negative dependence, but also strong, such as: Spain (−0.32), Finland (−0.66),
Italy (−0.43), Slovak Republic (−0.58), and Lithuania (−0.63). The negative
correlation can be explained by the fact that those countries have reduced
the level of restrictions while the economic support has been provided on
the same level.

To assess the influence of restrictions on confidence in economy of EU
citizens, we estimate the dependence between the Stringency Index and Economic Sentiment/Confidence Indicators. A monthly Economic Sentiment

Indicator (Eurostat, 2021f) is calculated on the basis of a selection of questions from industry, services, retail trade, construction, and consumers in order to track overall economic activity. It is made up of 15 individual components of the confidence indicators including industry (40%), services (30%), consumers (20%), construction (5%), and retail trade (5%). About 135,000 firms and some 32,000 consumers are currently surveyed every month across the EU (Eurostat, 2021f). Monthly Confidence Indicators (Eurostat, 2021f) reflect overall perceptions and expectations at the individual sector level in a one-dimensional index. Each confidence indicator is calculated as the simple arithmetic average of the (seasonally adjusted) balances of answers to specific questions chosen from the full set of questions in each individual survey (Eurostat, 2021f):

- The industrial confidence indicator – recent trends in production, the current levels of order books and stocks, expectations about production, selling prices and employment, capacity utilisation, and the number of months of production assured.
- The services confidence indicator – the managers' assessment of their recent business situation; the past and future changes in company's turnover and employment.
- The retail trade confidence indicator – recent developments in business situation, the current level of stocks, and expectations about a number of economic variables (production, new orders, and employment).
- The construction confidence – order book and employment expectations.
- The consumer confidence indicator – households' spending and savings intentions; the past and expected financial situation of households, the expected general economic situation and the intentions to make major purchases over the next 12 months.

The dependence between the level of restrictions and confidence in economy of EU citizens can be measured by assessing the Pearson correlation coefficient between Stringency Index and Economic Sentiment Indicators. The results of the study (Figure 3.7; Table 3.2) were obtained by using data from Eurostat and Oxford University for EU states between March 2020 and October 2021. Thus, we proved that the level of restrictions negatively correlates with Economic Sentiment and Confidence Indicators in all EU countries. In some of them, we can observe a highly strong negative dependence. Among these states are Belgium, Croatia, Cyprus, Denmark, Hungary, Ireland, Latvia, Lithuania, Luxembourg, Poland, Portugal, Romania, Slovak Republic, Slovenia, Spain, and Sweden. Moderate negative dependence is observed in Austria, Bulgaria, Estonia, Finland, France, Germany, Greece, Italy, Malta, and the Netherlands. In the Czech Republic, the level

Table 3.2 Pearson correlation between Stringency Index and Economic Sentiment/Confidence Indicators from March 2020 to October 2021 in EU states

	Economic sentiment indicator	Industrial confidence indicator	Services confidence indicator	Consumer confidence indicator	Construction confidence indicator	Retail confidence indicator	Unemployment expectations
Austria	−0.07	0.09	−0.14	−0.35	−0.01	−0.33	0.30
Belgium	**−0.60**	**−0.53**	**−0.66**	**−0.51**	**−0.66**	**−0.65**	**0.62**
Bulgaria	−0.36	−0.38	−0.28	−0.25	−0.41	−0.38	0.36
Croatia	**−0.59**	**−0.55**	**−0.57**	**−0.54**	**−0.58**	**−0.53**	0.28
Cyprus	**−0.71**	**−0.77**	**−0.66**	**−0.59**	−0.15	**−0.66**	**0.49**
Czech Republic	−0.25	0.06	−0.43	**−0.74**	−0.12	**−0.82**	**0.56**
Denmark	**−0.55**	**−0.49**	**−0.58**	**−0.49**	**−0.52**	**−0.41**	**0.45**
Estonia	**−0.50**	**−0.49**	−0.37	−0.27	−0.39	**−0.69**	**0.67**
Finland	−0.33	−0.21	−0.38	−0.40	−0.49	−0.32	0.39
France	**−0.45**	**−0.48**	−0.34	**−0.45**	−0.20	**−0.53**	0.11
Germany	−0.11	NDA	−0.31	−0.37	**−0.45**	−0.41	0.29
Greece	−0.29	−0.21	−0.27	**−0.48**	−0.06	−0.19	0.41
Hungary	**−0.71**	**−0.60**	**−0.77**	**−0.66**	**−0.45**	**−0.71**	**0.55**
Ireland	**−0.50**	**−0.50**	**−0.56**	−0.36	**−0.61**	**−0.56**	0.38
Italy	−0.41	−0.34	−0.43	**−0.57**	−0.26	**−0.55**	**0.62**
Latvia	**−0.61**	**−0.56**	**−0.66**	**−0.42**	**−0.62**	**−0.77**	**0.44**
Lithuania	−0.43	−0.37	−0.41	**−0.56**	−0.43	**−0.77**	**0.66**
Luxembourg	**−0.56**	**−0.58**	NDA	**−0.55**	−0.37	NDA	**0.47**
Malta	−0.24	−0.13	−0.34	−0.31	−0.44	−0.16	0.41
Netherlands	−0.38	−0.37	**−0.48**	−0.16	−0.25	**−0.74**	0.44
Poland	−0.46	−0.41	**−0.51**	**−0.55**	**−0.49**	**−0.62**	**0.67**
Portugal	**−0.50**	−0.43	**−0.56**	**−0.60**	**−0.59**	**−0.65**	**0.63**
Romania	**−0.56**	**−0.53**	**−0.55**	NDA	−0.43	−0.43	NDA
Slovak Republic	**−0.49**	−0.31	**−0.58**	**−0.51**	**−0.56**	**−0.58**	**0.53**
Slovenia	**−0.53**	−0.33	**−0.59**	**−0.68**	**−0.45**	**−0.68**	**0.65**
Spain	**−0.73**	**−0.63**	**−0.74**	**−0.70**	**−0.61**	**−0.80**	**0.73**
Sweden	**−0.45**	−0.44	**−0.50**	−0.23	**−0.77**	**−0.61**	**0.49**

Source: Authors' calculations based on data from Eurostat and daily data retrieved from https://data.humdata.org/event/covid-19.

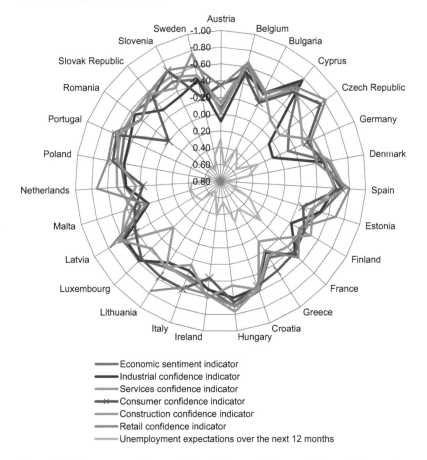

Austria
Sweden -1.00   Belgium
Slovenia   Bulgaria
-0.80
Slovak Republic -0.60   Cyprus
-0.40
Romania   -0.20   Czech Republic
0.00
Portugal   0.20   Germany
0.40
Poland   0.60   Denmark
0.80
Netherlands   Spain
Malta   Estonia
Latvia   Finland
Luxembourg   France
Lithuania   Greece
Italy   Croatia
Ireland   Hungary

───── Economic sentiment indicator
───── Industrial confidence indicator
───── Services confidence indicator
──×── Consumer confidence indicator
───── Construction confidence indicator
───── Retail confidence indicator
───── Unemployment expectations over the next 12 months

Figure 3.7 Pearson correlation coefficient between Stringency Index and Economic
Sentiment/Confidence Indicators from March 2020 to October 2021 in
EU states

Source: Authors' elaboration based on data from Eurostat and https://data.humdata.org/event/
covid-19.

of restrictions correlates with economic indicators in a moderate way, but
the dependence between restrictions and Consumer/Retail Confidence Indicators is strongly negative. So, we can conclude that the deterioration of the
economic situation in EU states has largely depended on the implemented
restrictions.

The next step of the study is to define the correlation between the level
of restrictions and the unemployment expectations over the next 12 months
(Table 3.2; Figure 3.7). The results show that unemployment expectations

highly depend on restrictions measures in EU countries. All estimates demonstrate the positive strong/moderate correlation between variables, which means that with an increase in lockdowns, there is also an increase of unemployment expectations.

The influence of measures such as income support, debt relief for households, fiscal measures, and support to other countries provided by governments of EU states on confidence in economy of EU citizens can be measured by assessing the Pearson correlation coefficient between Economic Support Index and Economic Sentiment/Confidence Indicators from April 2020 and October 2021 (Table 3.3; Figure 3.8). In some EU countries, it is possible to define the positive dependence between the Economic

Table 3.3 Pearson correlation between Economic Support Index and Economic Sentiment/Confidence Indicators from April 2020 to October 2021 for selected states of EU

	Austria	Spain	Finland	Greece	Italy	Lithuania	Poland	Slovak Republic
Economic sentiment indicator	**0.63**	0.41	**0.57**	0.34	0.47	0.36	**0.80**	**0.58**
Consumer confidence indicator	0.34	0.26	**0.64**	NDA	0.38	0.34	**0.59**	**0.73**
Industrial confidence indicator	**0.69**	0.48	0.44	0.38	0.46	0.34	**0.77**	0.31
Retail confidence indicator	0.35	NDA	NDA	0.19	**0.50**	**0.51**	**0.68**	**0.91**
Services confidence indicator	**0.65**	0.34	**0.62**	0.35	**0.50**	0.36	**0.82**	**0.69**
Construction confidence indicator	**0.59**	0.42	0.32	**0.71**	**0.57**	0.40	**0.82**	**0.90**
Unemployment expectations	−0.15	−0.27	**−0.52**	−0.44	−0.40	**−0.53**	**−0.67**	**−0.94**
Statement on financial situation of household	0.37	NDA	**0.49**	**0.51**	0.38	NDA	**0.62**	0.33

Source: Authors' calculations based on data from Eurostat and daily data retrieved from https://data.humdata.org/event/covid-19.

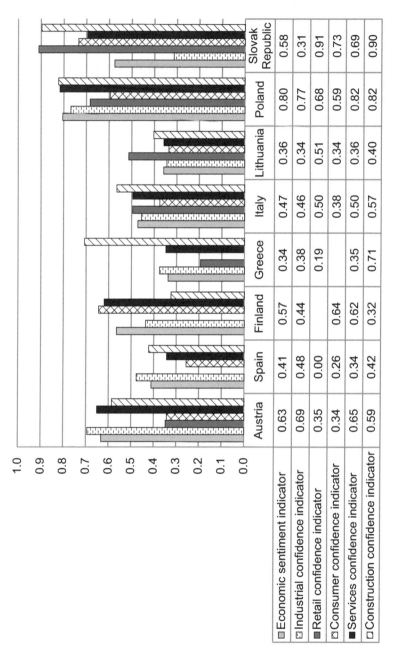

	Austria	Spain	Finland	Greece	Italy	Lithuania	Poland	Slovak Republic
Economic sentiment indicator	0.63	0.41	0.57	0.34	0.47	0.36	0.80	0.58
Industrial confidence indicator	0.69	0.48	0.44	0.38	0.46	0.34	0.77	0.31
Retail confidence indicator	0.35	0.00		0.19	0.50	0.51	0.68	0.91
Consumer confidence indicator	0.34	0.26	0.64		0.38	0.34	0.59	0.73
Services confidence indicator	0.65	0.34	0.62	0.35	0.50	0.36	0.82	0.69
Construction confidence indicator	0.59	0.42	0.32	0.71	0.57	0.40	0.82	0.90

Figure 3.8 Pearson correlation between Economic Support Index and Economic Sentiment/Confidence Indicators from April 2020 to October 2021 for selected states of EU

Source: Authors' calculations, based on data from Eurostat and daily data retrieved from https://data.humdata.org/event/covid-19.

Support Index and the Economic Sentiment/Confidence indicators between April 2020 and October 2021 (Table 3.3; Figure 3.8). Among these countries, stronger positive dependence is revealed in Austria, Finland, Poland, and Slovak Republic. A moderate correlation is observed in Spain, Greece, Italy, and Lithuania.

The average level of the Economic Support Index in Austria was 94.45 (Figure 3.5). Overall fiscal measures include (IMF, 2021) short-time working; a temporary reduction in the income tax rate, an additional negative tax for persons of low-income earners; special grants for SMEs, self-employed persons, freelancers, and artists; EUR 130 million to guarantee the supply of necessary medical equipment, corona aid fund (EUR 15 billion); state guarantee loans and grants to cover certain fixed costs within the State-Aid framework; specific tax reliefs for hospitality sectors; deferral of corporate taxes, VAT and income taxes; investment premium with additional incentives for investment projects in health, environment, and digitalisation; EUR 700 million to cover short-term costs in sport and culture; EUR 25 million for Austrian film industry; and EUR 500 million – tax reductions and government investment in forestry sectors with the ultimate goal to reduce the use of fossil fuels in this sector. This support highly correlates with economic situation (0.63), industry (0.69), services (0.65), and construction (0.59) as well as retail (0.35) and consumer's confidence (0.34) (Table 3.3). Thus, the restrictions on the average level of 61.06 (Table 3.2) have been mitigated by fiscal measures contributing to improvement of the economic situation.

The Economic support in Spain was also high (87.35) compared to other EU states (Figure 3.5). Overall fiscal measures include about 7.4% of GDP (EUR 85 billion) (IMF, 2021), i.e.: budget support to health services; entitlement of unemployment benefit for workers temporarily laid off under the Temporary Employment Adjustment Schemes due to COVID-19; measures taken by regional governments on social services, education and support to firms; direct aid for corporate solvency support an extraordinary benefit for self-employed workers; introduction of a new means-tested Minimum Income Scheme; investment in digitisation and innovation in the tourism sector; a temporary subsidy for household employees affected by COVID-19; transfer of EUR 25 million to autonomous communities funding meals for children affected by the school closure; extension of the social benefit for energy provision and other industry and sectoral support measures; exemptions of social contributions for impacted companies and self-employed; temporary zero VAT rate on purchases of medical material essential to combat the COVID-19; deferral of social security debts for companies and the self-employed; moratoria of social security contributions for the self-employed and companies in selected industries; tax payment deferrals for small and medium enterprises and self-employed; budget flexibility to enable transfers between budget lines and for local governments to use budget surplus from the previous years for supporting measures in the area of housing; and an emergency management process for the procurement of all goods and services needed by the public sector to implement any measure to address COVID-19. According to results of the study, the dependence between industrial and construction confidence indicators and economic support is above 0.4 (Table 3.3; Figure 3.8). In general, the Economic Sentiment Indicator correlates with the Economic Support Index on the level of 0.41 (Table 3.3). Unfortunately, despite the support, the negative effects of restrictions had a severe impact on the economy. The correlation of all Confidence Indicators with Stringency Index is on the level between 0.7 and 0.8 (Table 3.2).

The average Economic Support Index in Finland was on the level of 72.19 (Figure 3.5). Key spending measures (around 3% of GDP) include healthcare and testing, protection and medical equipment, public safety and border controls, research on the coronavirus epidemic; grants to SMEs and self-employed; and expanded parental allowance, social assistance, and unemployment insurance (IMF, 2021). Supplementary budget proposals for 2020 included (IMF, 2021): an additional EUR 1.2 billion in support to households and businesses; increased public investment (EUR 1.2 billion); EUR 60 million to support the most vulnerable in society; an increase of EUR 1 billion in revenue estimates due to less than anticipated use of flexible tax-related payment arrangement introduced to support liquidity; EUR 200 million to support the rapid increase in cross-border testing capacity and analysis as part of the hybrid strategy for cross-border traffic and travel; EUR 750 million to municipalities for implementing the hybrid testing and tracing strategy and basic public services; EUR 200 million to the country's hospital districts for pandemic-related costs; and EUR 90 million for the acquisition of COVID-19 vaccines. A government proposal to amend the 2021 budget includes EUR 350 million in capital funding for Finavia Corporation; EUR 56 million for unemployment security; and EUR 45 million to increase the health insurance reimbursements for COVID19 tests carried about by private healthcare providers (IMF, 2021). On May 18, 2021, parliament approved the EU's proposed financing of its Recovery and Resilience Facility. According to the plan, Finland is expected to receive roughly EUR 2.1 billion over 2021–2026, among others for the green transition (around 51%) and digital transformation projects (24%). On June 23, 2021, the government announced that temporary amendments to business development aid will continue till the end of 2021, with a company-specific maximum state aid of EUR 1.8 million (IMF, 2021).

On the basis of Pearson correlation, we could observe a strong positive dependence between the Economic Support Index and the Economic

Sentiment/Confidence Indicators between April 2020 and October 2021 (Table 3.3; Figure 3.8). Consumer and services confidence indicators have the strongest dependence (0.64 and 0.62, respectively) with the Economic Support Index. The dependence between the Economic Sentiment Indicator and Economic Support Index is 0.57 (Table 3.3). Taking into account the results of the correlation between the Stringency Index and the Economic Sentiment/Confidence Indicators, the influence of restrictions on the economy was not too hard, or in other words, the influence of restrictions have been mitigated by economic support.

The average Economic Support Index in Greece was 80.79 (Figure 3.5). The government implemented a fiscal package of measures totalling about 13.7% of GDP (EUR 23.5 billion) in 2020, including loan guarantees, financed from national and EU resources. Key measures included (IMF, 2021) health spending for hiring doctors and nurses, procurement of medical supplies, and cash bonuses to health sector workers; temporary transfers to vulnerable individuals, including cash stipends and full coverage of pension and health benefit payments for employees working in hard hit firms and for self-employed professionals, extension of unemployment benefits, support for short-term employment, subsidies to households loans tied to their primary residency, and paid leave for parents who have children not going to school; liquidity support to hard hit businesses through loan guarantees, loan, and interest payment subsidies, refundable advance payment, rent reductions, and deferred payments of taxes and social security contributions; and VAT rate reductions for critical products needed for COVID-19 protection, research spending, and transportation and hospitality sectors. The government extended selected support measures in parallel to the imposition of new movement restrictions in November 2020 and March 2021, increasing the cost of fiscal measures to about 8.5% of GDP in 2021.

The highest dependence between the Economic Support Index and Sentiment Indicators is observed in construction (0.71) (Table 3.3; Figure 3.8). The positive activity is further boosted by Greek government decisions to facilitate private sector investments. Greece's construction industry registered growth in 2020, despite the lockdown measures imposed by the government. According to the Hellenic Statistical Authority, the construction industry's value adds at seasonally adjusted terms grew by 14.3% year on year in the first quarter of 2021 and was preceded by year-on-year growth rates of 0.6% in the fourth quarter, 12.1% in the third, and 24% in the second quarter of 2020 (Global Information Inc., 2021). An increase in building permits and foreign direct investment in construction will also contribute to the industry's growth momentum in the early part of the forecast period. The government is focusing on the development of renewable energy projects, in line with its target to increase the share of renewable energy in the total energy mix by 35% over the next 10 years (Global Information Inc., 2021).

The average Economic Support Index in Italy was 72.32 (Figure 3.5). The Economic Sentiment/Confidence Indicators correlates with the Economic Support Index on average level of 0.5 (Table 3.3; Figure 3.8) revealing strong positive dependence. Considering fiscal measures, the "Cura Italia" emergency package (EUR 25 billion or 1.6% of GDP) included funds to strengthen the Italian health care system and civil protection; measures to preserve jobs and support income of laid-off workers and self-employed; other measures to support businesses, including tax deferrals and post-ponement of utility bill payments in most affected municipalities; as well as measures to support credit supply (IMF, 2021). The Liquidity Decree allowed for additional state guarantees of up to EUR 400 billion (25% of GDP) aimed to unlock more than EUR 750 billion (close to 50% of GDP) of liquidity for businesses and households. "Relaunch" package of fiscal measures (EUR 55 billion or 3.5% of GDP) provided further income sup-port for families, funds for the healthcare system, and other measures to sup-port businesses, including grants for SMEs and tax deferrals (IMF, 2021). On October 27, 2020, the government adopted a EUR 5.4 billion (0.3% of GDP) package for quick relief to the sectors affected by the latest round of COVID-19 containment actions. Measures include grants to 460,000 SMEs and the self-employed, and further income support for families. The gov-ernment has also extended social contribution exemptions for affected busi-nesses. On March 19 and May 20, 2021, the government approved further support packages for about EUR 72 billion aiming at extending supports for business and workers affected by the pandemic as well as kickstarting the economy [i.e. compensating businesses and the self-employed (proportional to 2020 turnover loss) and extending the firing ban (until end-June) and the short-time work schemes] (IMF, 2021).

The average Economic Support Index in the Republic of Lithuania was 73.32 (Figure 3.5). The restrictions have influenced retail the most (−0.77) (Table 3.2; Figure 3.6). On the other hand, considering Pearson correlation between Economic Support Index and Economic Sentiment/Confidence Indicators, the strongest dependence is with Retail Indicator (0.51) (Table 3.3; Figure 3.8). Other indicators correlate with the Economic Support Index on the level of 0.3 (Table 3.3; Figure 3.8). Thus, economic support has been correctly directed to the most affected sector. According to the IMF (2021), on March 16, 2020, the government announced an overall fiscal package of EUR 2.5 billion (5% of GDP) including additional funds for the health-care system and emergency management; additional funds for caring for the sick and disabled, support for the self-employed, and wage subsidies for employees in affected firms; and co-financing of climate change investment projects. In addition, the government expanded guarantee schemes, including guarantees for agricultural as well as SME loans by around EUR 1.3 billion; provided interest compensation support for SME's with deferred loans, a new financial instrument for businesses to form portfolios from business loans, cheap loans targeted to hard hit sectors like travel services and accommodation and services, and increased financial support to the agricultural sector. On May 7, 2020, the government approved to support an economic recovery for businesses and households. The package includes extended wage subsidies for persons returning from downtime or unemployment, job search allowances of EUR 200 for those who have dropped out of the labour force, an increase in social benefits to pensioners and others, additional funds for the self-employed and for vocational training, and an increase in unemployment benefits. An investment plan comprising EUR 6.3 billion (13% of 2019 GDP) for new and already planned investment that will be accelerated.

In the government's 2021 budget, EUR 1.1 billion was allocated to economic support measures during the second quarantine including an extension of wage subsidies, job search allowances, interest expense compensation, soft loans to businesses, and funds for the acquisition of COVID-19 vaccines (IMF, 2021). Additional targeted measures were later introduced including extra subsidies for businesses with the largest drop in sales due to national quarantine restrictions. The national budget has since been revised, and additional funds were allocated for health and labour market measures.

The average Economic Support Index in Poland was 68.05 (Figure 3.5). Economic Sentiment Indicator strongly correlates with Economic Support Index on the level of 0.8 (Figure 3.8). In general, all economic indicators highly depend on economic support (i.e. Industrial Confidence Indicator −0.77; Retail Confidence Indicator −0.68; Consumer Confidence Indicator −0.59; Services and Construction Confidence Indicators −0.82) (Table 3.3; Figure 3.8). Meanwhile, the highest influence of restrictions was in services (−0.51), consumer confidence (−0.55) and retail (−0.62) (Table 3.2; Figure 3.7).

The fiscal policy response to the first wave of the pandemic was sizable, estimated at PLN 116 billion (5.2% of GDP). It includes new credit guarantees and micro-loans for entrepreneurs estimated at PLN 74 billion (3.3% of GDP) and a liquidity programme for businesses at PLN 100 billion (4.5% of GDP). Most of the measures have expired by now. Among other key measures: additional funds for hospital equipment and supplies; wage subsidies for employees of affected businesses and self-employed persons; increased guarantees from the national development bank for medium and large companies; additional loans for micro-firms; postponement or cancellation of social insurance contributions; an allowance for parents of young children related to school closures; a "solidarity benefit" for those who lost jobs after March 15, paid for three months (June–August); an increase in the unemployment benefit by 39% during the first 90 days of unemployment (IMF, 2021). Additionally, establishment of a new COVID-19 fund dedicated to combat the negative impact of the pandemic with the balance sheet size of PLN 100 billion; financial support of the investment tasks managed by local governments; interest rate subsidies for bank loans granted to provide financial liquidity to entrepreneurs affected by the COVID-19; additional support for public investment in road and railway infrastructure, as well as PLN 1 billion to support operational situation of companies managing airports (IMF, 2021).

In response to the second wave of the pandemic, the anti-crisis shield 6.0 was approved by the president. The additional fiscal measures are targeted to the most affected sectors of the economy and include exemptions from social security contributions, subsidised loans, wage subsidies, and benefits for self-employed. The estimated cost of such support is around 1.7% of GDP. Given the deteriorating pandemic situation during the third wave of COVID-19, these measures were consequently extended for new branches and prolonged for March and April, i.e. co-financing of fixed costs for SMEs in the industries most affected by the restrictions; subsidies under the PFR Financial Shield; writing off of the subsidies and the repayable part of the PFR liquidity loans to micro-firms and SMEs; extension of the Financial Shield programme for large companies; change in the rules for calculating the damage due to COVID-19 in preferential loans from the current March–August 2020 to March 2020–March 2021, in accordance with the original shape of the programme. In general, according to preliminary government estimates, the above-the-line fiscal cost of anti-crisis measures amounted to 4.25% of GDP in 2020.

The average Economic Support Index in the Slovak Republic was 91.24 (Figure 3.5). Based on Pearson coefficients, restrictions have highly influenced the economy. Almost all coefficients are nearly on the level of 0.5 (Table 3.2, Figure 3.7). On the other hand, all economic indicators highly depend on economic support (i.e. Retail and Construction Confidence Indicators −0.9; Consumer Confidence Indicator −0.73; Services Confidence Indicator −0.69; Economic Sentiment Indicator −0.58 and Industrial Confidence Indicator −0.31) (Table 3.3; Figure 3.8). This means that fiscal measures have contributed to a large extent to minimise the effects of pandemic. Measures introduced by the coalition government include (IMF, 2021): wage compensation for affected businesses and self-employed, and subsidies to individuals without income; enhanced unemployment benefits, and sickness and nursing benefits; deferral and waiver of employers' social security contributions for some months for affected companies and self-employed (deferral extended to September 2023); easing of the administrative burden on businesses and relaxing labour code requirements; deferral of payroll and corporate tax payments for businesses whose revenues decline by more than 40%; rental subsidies; and higher medical spending. Total disbursed above-the-line measures in 2020 amounted to EUR 1.9 billion (2.1% of GDP) and contributed to the widening of the fiscal deficit to 6.1% of GDP. In addition to policies with direct fiscal impact, the government introduced several measures to ease liquidity pressures. A number of state-guarantee schemes were launched, up to a total of EUR 4 billion or 4.4% of 2020 GDP, covering both SMEs and large firms, though intake amounted to 1.04 billion in 2020. Individuals, self-employed, and SMEs are also allowed to defer loan repayments for up to 9 months (application deadline later extended to March 2021), while a rent payment moratorium was imposed until June 30, 2020. The government also introduced temporary state protection from creditors for affected businesses.

The 2021 revised budget included in the Stability Programme includes funds/reserve allocated to COVID-19 response amounting to 4.2% of GDP (3.4 billion direct aid and 0.6 billion below-the-line measures) and envisages a fiscal deficit of 9.9% of GDP in 2021 (IMF, 2021).

3.4   Medium- to long-term economic trends in the EU

Epidemiologists suggest that the global world is faced mainly with threats related to diseases affecting currently developed societies, the so-called civilisation diseases such as cancer, diabetes, and diseases caused by sedentary lifestyle. The other threat for the future existence of humanity is new infectious diseases, taking the form of a pandemic and very costly to combat. The "Spanish flu" pandemic (the influenza pandemic) of 1918–1919 is an excellent example which fully reflects a state of matter. Thus, we would like to present economic effects of the influenza pandemic briefly, which could be a close analogue to the current crisis because (a) the 1918 virus was also a "novel" virus; (b) like COVID-19, no one had immunity to it, and it was highly infectious, spreading through respiratory droplets that pass when an infected person coughed or sneezed; (c) several cities implemented mask mandates, describing them as a symbol of "wartime patriotism," but some people refused to comply or take them seriously (Lovelace, 2020); (d) it was the most severe pandemic in recent history. It covered three waves and killed 50 million people worldwide from 1918 through 1919, including 675,000 Americans, according to the Centers for Disease Control and Prevention (CDC, 2019). It is estimated that one-third of the world's population became infected with the virus. The first wave came with the usual flu symptoms. The second wave was dramatically worse. It could set in suddenly, killing patients within days or even hours. The virus would cause their lungs to fill with fluid and the lack of oxygen would make their skin turn blue until they suffocated (Lovelace, 2020).

While much has been written about the medical causes of the Spanish flu, limited attention has been given to the economic effects of the epidemic which allow for providing predictions concerning long-term economic outcomes of COVID-19 in modern times and establishing appropriate policy responses. The greatest disadvantage of studying the economic effects of the 1918 influenza is the lack of reliable economic data from the time period. The second one concerns the fact that the flu occurred during and shortly after World War I.

The large economic disruption due to the epidemic could be found in contemporaneous newspapers. The Wall Street Journal, on October 24, 1918, wrote:

> In some parts of the country [the pandemic] has caused a decrease in production of approximately 50% and almost everywhere it has occasioned more or less falling off. The loss of trade which the retail merchants throughout the country have met with has been very large. The impairment of efficiency has also been noticeable. There never has been in this country, so the experts say, so complete domination by an epidemic as has been the case with this one.
>
> (Correia et al. 2020, p.11).

In contemporary scientific discourse, we can find some academic studies that have looked at the economic effects of pandemics using available data. Three cases can illustrate some of the possible outcomes in a rapid-onset pandemic: a mild case (as in the 1968 flu pandemic, cost of 0.7% of GDP), a moderate case (as in the 1958 flu pandemic, cost of 3.1% of GDP), and a severe case (as in the case of the 1918 pandemic, cost of 4.8% of GDP) (Burns et al., 2008).

Considering short-run costs, it will be appropriate to indicate the recent research concerning the Spanish Influenza Pandemic of Barro et al. (2020). They estimated that the Spanish Flu between 1918 and 1920 resulted in the death of 39 million people globally (a death rate of 2% of the entire population). Authors revealed that the pandemic was responsible for reducing real GDP per capita and real private consumption per capita in the particular country by 6% and 8%, respectively. Brainerd and Siegler (2003) analysed the influence of the influenza on economic growth. Studying changes in real personal incomes between 1919/21 and 1930, they revealed that the United States experienced a significantly higher income growth rate from the onset of the influenza to 1930. Meanwhile, Karlsson et al. (2014), providing the comparative analysis, state that, there is virtually no correlation between sectoral composition and Spanish flu mortality, suggesting that the spread of the influenza virus was largely unrelated to initial regional economic conditions.

Talking about the long-term effect of the 1918 influenza, we can mention the work of Almond (2006). The study is based on the reviewed evidence that suggested pregnant women who were exposed to the influenza in 1918 gave birth to children who had greater medical problems later in life, such as schizophrenia, diabetes, and stroke. The author states that an individual's health is positively related to the human capital and productivity and thus wages and income. Using 1960–1980 decennial census data, the author found that "men and women show large and discontinuous reductions in educational attainment if they had been in utero during the pandemic. The children of infected mothers were up to 15% less likely to graduate from high school. Wages of men were 5%–9% lower because of infection" (Almond, 2006). Moreover, historical and medical records suggest deterioration in health (e.g. chronic bronchitis, drowsiness, and sleeping sickness) among some survivors after the Spanish flu in later life (see e.g. Collier, 1996; Ravenholt & Foege, 1982).

Barro et al. (2020) attempt to draw implications from the Spanish Flu for the current COVID-19 crisis. They suggest that the 1918–20 pandemic could be regarded as a worst-case scenario. In this case, a death rate of 2% today would amount to 150 million deaths worldwide, and the decline in material living standards would be 6%–8%. They state that "the large potential losses in lives and economic activity justify substantial expenditure of resources to attempt to limit the damage" and reflect that "countries have been pursuing a policy of lowering real GDP . . . as a way of curbing the spread of the disease" (Barro et al., 2020, p. 17). Scientists conclude that there is clearly a difficult trade-off here concerning lives versus material goods, with very little discussion about how this trade-off should be assessed and acted upon.

The 1918 flu pandemic reveals that individual and community responses are linked with preparedness, level of knowledge, communications by the authorities, public trust, and public health measures. Failures could be reflected in the provision of public and private goods and services (like security, health, food, water, transport, banking, communications, etc.) at the local, national, and international levels.

Scenarios regarding how the EU economy will recover after the current shock will depend on the way the pandemic will end. There are two perspectives – the pandemic will subside either rapidly (as in the case of Spanish flu) or gradually, over a longer period. In the modern, highly globalised world of trade and capital movements, the shocks would propagate across interconnected economic and financial systems worldwide. The evolution of a pandemic in any one country or community is largely unpredictable, but we make an attempt to present the effects of pandemic in a short-run perspective and predict potential economic effects in a long-run perspective (Figure 3.9).

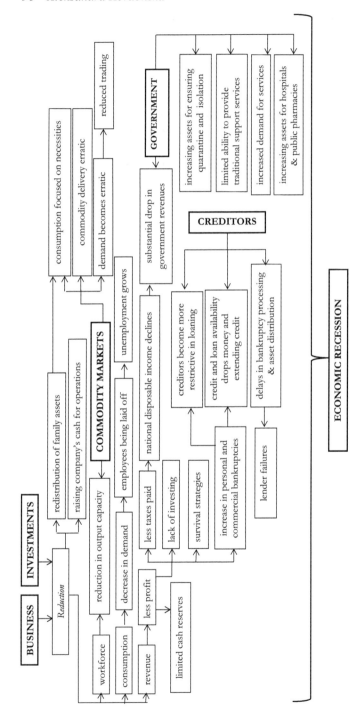

Figure 3.9 Potential economic effects of COVID-19 in short- and long-term perspectives

Source: Authors' own elaboration.

Anyway, people have experienced economic downturn associated with shifts in demand, supply shocks, economic, and social disruptions. It is caused by isolation and quarantine regime aimed at reducing interpersonal contacts. On the one hand, a rise in bank charge-offs reflects an increase in business and household defaults. Besides, many businesses in the service and entertainment industries have suffered huge losses in revenue, while businesses that specialised in healthcare products have experienced an increase. The negative impact is observed in services sectors such as tourism, retail trade, transport, and entertainment. Public health measures and quarantine in accordance to prevent illness also have had economic costs. The direct (medication and hospitalisation) and indirect (production losses) costs have arisen, associated with human illness and death. Production losses have come from the workers' death, illness, or staying home for quarantine. It results in a supply shock. This has disrupted labour-intensive sectors the most (such as public order, transport, education, health care, and retail commerce in food and non-food goods) and networked industries (such as banking, utilities, and communications) (see, e.g. Blenkinsop 2020).

One may wonder which actions should be taken by the European community in order to revive the economy as fast as possible after COVID-19 pandemic. The EU response to the pandemic crisis has been innovative.

The EU has provided collective actions such as (European Council 2020; Eurostat, 2021e):

1   Measures adopted as a part of 2014–2020 Multiannual Financial Framework;
2   EUR 200 billion Pan-European guarantee fund for loans provided by the European Investment Bank to enterprises;
3   EUR 240 billion support from the European Stability Mechanism for countries;
4   €100 billion support to citizens via the new Unemployment Risks in an Emergency instrument;
5   EUR 37 billion Coronavirus Response Investment Initiative Packages (CRII and CRII+);
6   EUR 750 billion Pandemic Emergency Purchase Programme from the European Central Bank aimed at expanding the range of eligible assets under the corporate sector purchase programme and providing the benefits for all sectors of the economy that enable them to absorb the COVID-19 shock;
7   EUR 1 billion to R&I in the health sector under Horizon 2020; and
8   EUR 800 million of direct support for the healthcare sector from the EU Solidarity Fund.

Monetary support was also promptly provided. As the current crisis has a major impact on public finances, the European Commission has activated the general escape clause of the Stability and Growth Pact. The clause allows national fiscal policies to support the economy more freely by full flexibility foreseen under State aid rules and an extension of the deadline for the Member States to correct their excessive deficits under the excessive deficit procedure. National governments also agreed for the first time on common debt issuance to finance an EU economic recovery plan, Next Generation EU. These measures as well as drop in GDP resulted in the EU's government deficit-to-GDP ratio which increased from −0.5% in 2019 to −6.9% in 2020 (Eurostat, 2021g).

The way the EU will get through the crisis depends on many factors like the effectiveness of pandemic control and successful implementation of recovery programs (See, e.g. Hutt, 2020; OECD, 2021a; UNnews 2020). As to the European Commission (2021a), the EU economy already faced several long-term structural challenges before the COVID-19 crisis, such as rapidly ageing population threatened to eventually reduce labour supply; weak productivity growth compared to China and the United States in the process of digital transformation; very substantial socio-economic costs of climate change; and rising income and wealth inequality, territorial disparities within and among Member States, and unequal access to education and skills. So, the COVID-19 made these challenges more visible and more relevant.

As of November 2021, only 54% of people living in Europe are fully vaccinated. Today Europe is divided between countries which have imposed COVID-19 restrictions on unvaccinated citizens (like Germany, Austria, and Slovakia) to tackle a fourth wave of the pandemic and those which have not (like France and Poland). On the one hand, strict public health measures could lead to wider social and economic crisis (i.e. economic downturn, unemployment, curtailed civil liberties). On the other hand, assuming a situation where the vaccine is effective but governments focus on keeping the economy open, thus consumer confidence fades and these initiatives however fail. Five scenarios are presented by European Commission (2021b) based on interdependencies and sensitivities. In our opinion, even in the case of partially effective vaccine, transparent and evidence-based communication, citizens' active engagement, and cooperation with government can lead to protective immunity in the population.

The key recommendations on the recovery measures and policies are:

1   EU recovery and resilience plans should consider the specificities of the industrial issue and develop the competitiveness of the EU industry via investments in R&D and digital re/upskilling;
2   The transition towards climate neutrality and a circular economy will enhance well-being and open major opportunities for improving European industrial strengths (OECD, 2021c);

3   To avoid the rise of regional inequalities, poorer regions need to improve their productive specialisation. For that purpose, cohesion and rural development policies need to be revamped to gain in efficiency, notably by supporting more effectively innovation (OECD, 2021c);

4   Persistent fiscal divergence between Member States should be mitigated by reduction of high and divergent public debt ratios in a sustainable, growth-friendly manner (Verwey & Monks, 2021);

5   Reinforcing counter-cyclicality in the EU fiscal framework could strengthen the medium-term dimension of fiscal policy and thus the ability of national fiscal policy to respond to economic fluctuations (Verwey & Monks, 2021);

6   EU countries should foster public and private investment, especially to improve European interconnections, and increase cross-country collaboration in innovative industrial projects, including healthcare;

7   Preventing and correcting macroeconomic imbalances enhances Member States' ability to respond to shocks and supports economic convergence;

8   The need for transparent and evidence-based communication between government and citizens will continue to be critical to secure public trust and facilitate cooperation by the majority of the population with the tough measures necessary for rebuilding (European Commission, 2021b);

9   The pandemic has confirmed the critical importance and power of collaboration: sustainability and resilience will require scale and coordination at the EU level (European Commission, 2021b)

References

Almond, D. (2006). Is the 1918 influenza pandemic over? Long-term effect of in utero influenza exposure in the post-1940 U.S. population. *Journal of Political Economy*, *114*(4), 672–712. https://doi.org/10.1086/507154

Atlantic Council. (2020). *Can we compare the COVID-19 and 2008 crises?* www.atlanticcouncil.org/blogs/new-atlanticist/can-we-compare-the-covid-19-and-2008-crises/

Barro, J., Ursua, J. F., & Weng, J. (2020). The coronavirus and the Great Influenza Pandemic: Lessons from the "Spanish Flu" for the coronavirus's potential effects on mortality and economic activity. *CESifo Working Paper Series No. 8166, CESifo Group Munich.* www.cesifo.org

Blenkinsop, P. (2020). Coronavirus could reduce world trade by up to a third, according to the WTO. *World Economic Forum.* www.weforum.org

Bordo, M., & Sinha, A. (2016). A lesson from The Great Depression that the fed might have learned: A comparison of the 1932 open market purchases with quantitative easing. *NBER Working Paper No. 22581.* www.nber.org/papers/w22581

Brainerd, E., & Siegler, M. (2003). The economic effects of the 1918 influenza epidemic. *CEPR Discussion Papers No. 3791.* www.cepr.org/active/publications/discussion_papers/dp.php?dpno=3791

Burns, A., van der Mensbrugghe, D., & Timmer, H. (2008). Evaluating the economic consequences of avian influenza. *World Bank.* www.worldbank.org/flu

CDC. (2019). *Past pandemics, pandemic influenza.* Retrieved from www.cdc.gov/flu/pandemic-resources/1918-pandemic-h1n1.html

Collier, R. (1996). *The plague of the Spanish lady: The influenza pandemic of 1918–1919.* Allison&Busby.

Correia, S., Luck, S., & Verner, E. (2020). Pandemics depress the economy, public health interventions do not: Evidence from the 1918 flu. *SSRN.* http://dx.doi.org/10.2139/ssrn.3561560

De Vet, J. M., Nigohosyan, D., Nunez Ferrer, J., Gross, A.-K., Kuehl, S., & Flickenschild, M. (2021). Impacts of the COVID-19 pandemic on EU industries. *European Parliament.* www.europarl.europa.eu/RegData/etudes/STUD/2021/662903/IPOL_STU(2021)662903_EN.pdf

European Commission. (2021a). The EU economy after COVID-19: Implications for economic governance. *Communication from The Commission to The European Parliament, The Council, The European Central Bank, The European Economic and Social Committee, The Committee of The Regions.* https://ec.europa.eu/info/sites/default/files/economy-finance/economic_governance_review-communication.pdf

European Commission. (2021b). The scientific, technological and societal conditions for the end of the COVID-19 crisis. *Publications Office of the European Union.* http://dx.doi.org/10.2777/293413

European Council. (2020). *Report on the comprehensive economic policy response to the COVID-19 pandemic.* www.consilium.europa.eu

Eurostat. (2020a). *Impact of COVID-19 on main GDP aggregates including employment* (2020, July 20). https://ec.europa.eu/eurostat/statistics-explained/

Eurostat. (2021a). *Contributions of each institutional sector to macroeconomic developments charts* [Data set]. https://ec.europa.eu/eurostat/web/sector-accounts/detailed-charts/contributions-sectors

Eurostat. (2021b). *European statistical recovery dashboard* (2021, November) [Data set]. https://ec.europa.eu/eurostat/cache/recovery-dashboard/

Eurostat. (2021c). *Impact of Covid-19 crisis on industrial production* (2021, September). https://ec.europa.eu/eurostat/statistics-explained/

Eurostat. (2021d). *Impact of Covid-19 crisis on non-financial corporation and household accounts* (2021, May). https://ec.europa.eu/eurostat/statistics-explained/

Eurostat. (2021e). *Jobs and economy during the coronavirus pandemic.* https://ec.europa.eu/info/live-work-travel-eu/coronavirus-response/jobs-and-economy-during-coronavirus-pandemic_en

Eurostat. (2021f). Business and consumer surveys. *Data Description.* https://ec.europa.eu/eurostat/cache/metadata/en/ei_bcs_esms.htm

Eurostat. (2021g). *Government finance statistics* (2021, October 20). https://ec.europa.eu/eurostat/statistics-explained/index.php?title=Government_finance_statistics

Global Information Inc. (2021, September 14). *Market research report. Construction in Greece – key trends and opportunities to 2025 (H2 2021)*. www.giiresearch.com/report/gd268675-construction-greece-key-trends-opportunities.html

Hutt, R. (2020). Act fast and do whatever it takes' to fight the COVID-19 crisis', say leading economists. *World Economic Forum.* www.weforum.org

IMF. (2021). *Policy responses to COVID-19* (Last updated on 2021, July 2). www.imf.org/en/Topics/imf-and-covid19/Policy-Responses-to-COVID-19#S

Karlsson, M., Nilsson, T., & Pichler, S. (2014). The impact of the 1918 Spanish flu epidemic on economic performance in Sweden: An investigation into the consequences of an extraordinary mortality shock. *Journal of Health Economics, 36,* 1–19. https://doi.org/10.1016/j.jhealeco.2014.03.005

Lovelace, B. Jr. (2020). Medical historian compares the coronavirus to the 1918 flu pandemic: Both were highly political. *CNBC.* www.cnbc.com/2020/09/28/comparing-1918-flu-vs-coronavirus.html

OECD. (2020a). *Evaluating the initial impact of COVID-19 containment measures on economic activity* (2020, June 10). www.oecd.org/coronavirus/policy-responses/evaluating-the-initial-impact-of-covid-19-containment-measures-on-economic-activity-b1f6b68b/

OECD. (2020b). *OECD policy responses to coronavirus (COVID-19). Corporate sector vulnerabilities during the Covid-19 outbreak: Assessment and policy responses* (2020, May 5). www.oecd.org/coronavirus/policy-responses/corporate-sector-vulnerabilities-during-the-covid-19-outbreak-assessment-and-policy-responses-a6e670ea/

OECD. (2021a). Keeping The recovery on track. *OECD Economic Outlook, Interim Report* (2021, September). www.oecd-ilibrary.org/sites/490d4832-en/index.html?itemId=/content/publication/490d4832-en

OECD. (2021b). *OECD COVID-19 recovery dashboard* [Data set]. www.oecd.org/coronavirus/en/recovery-dashboard

OECD. (2021c). *OECD economic surveys: European Union 2021. Executive Summary.* https://doi.org/10.1787/3d5fc1b4-en

OECD. (2021d). *OECD economic surveys: European Union 2021. Key policy insights.* https://doi.org/10.1787/5dc83bf6-en

Ravenholt, R., & Foege, W. (1982). 1918 influenza, encephalitis lethargica, parkinsonism. *The Lancet, 320*(8303), 860–864.

Ritchie, H., Mathieu, E., Rodés-Guirao, L., Appel, C., Giattino, Ch., Ortiz-Ospina, E., Hasell, J., Macdonald, B., Beltekian, D., & Roser, M. (2020). *Coronavirus pandemic (COVID-19).* https://ourworldindata.org/coronavirus

UNnews. (2020). *UN launches COVID-19 plan that could 'defeat the virus and build a better world.* https://news.un.org

Verwey, M., & Monks, A. (2021). *The EU economy after COVID-19: Implications for economic governance.* https://voxeu.org/article/eu-economy-after-covid-19-implications-economic-governance

Postface

The COVID-19 pandemic is undoubtedly a major challenge for the EU Member States. It has challenged them to protect the lives and health of their citizens. At the beginning of the pandemic, each of the countries faced the problem of lack of knowledge about the threat and the need for developed instruments, which, together with the limited capacity of health care systems, resulted in a significant increase in the incidence of the disease. A number of actions taken by the Member States were an attempt to find effective solutions.

The research carried out in Chapter 1 oscillated around the analysis of the "covidian" policy of the EU Member States, using the research tool Governments Policy COVID Index [GPCI]. The review of restrictions applied by the states to COVID-19 allowed to extract a catalogue of instruments, which in the following parts served as X indicators for GPCI (legal measures, masks, remote schooling, remote working, international movement restrictions, national movement restrictions and public meetings limitations, shop closing, catering and hotels, and public transport restrictions) for case study analysis. For the purpose of the study, a typology was created, taking into account three approaches to government response to COVID-19 in the context of the strength of the impact of the introduced restrictions.

The research problem revolved around the question to what extent the "covidian" policy applied by the countries had an individual character and to what extent the EU countries relied on a common catalogue of solutions? The main hypothesis was adopted as the statement, that the "covidian" policy of EU countries to a large extent had an individual character, through individual search for solutions by individual member states depending on the epidemiological situation in the country. The working hypothesis was also applied that the policy of EU countries to a large extent had a common character, through the application of similar solutions. On the basis of the research, it can be concluded that the policies applied by EU countries were to a large extent based on similar instruments, and although each country

DOI: 10.4324/9781003222538-4

introduced restrictions and determined the direction of action on its own, these instruments did not differ significantly. The differentiating factor in this context was their specificity and method of implementation in the country. Therefore, it can be concluded that the hypothesis was not confirmed, in this case, the assumption proved correct.

The exception among the 28 countries surveyed was Sweden, with the GPCI score of 9, which largely adopted a different approach to the policy applied. Most of the actions taken were not restrictions but recommendations. Sweden's COVID-19 pandemic control strategy was based on the key objectives of explicitly reducing human migration rather than suppressing it through prohibitions and restrictions. The focus was on protecting the group most at risk of severe disease (the sick and elderly) rather than restricting all citizens. It was recognised that closing schools and universities could do more harm to children and adolescents than getting infected with COVID-19. Sweden focused on ensuring that health resources and medical care were available in all regions and that health care was not strained. Great attention has been paid to alleviating public concerns by communicating with residents through official information on websites and regular press conferences (Swedish-Government, Strategy, 2020). In Sweden, an extremely important factor in being "comfortable" with a pandemic was the fact that the country's health service, in terms of access to medical services and quality of care, was among the best in Europe. Also important is the low population density, which has allowed the country to maintain social distance without restrictions (Jonung, 2020; Karlson, Stern & Klein, 2020; Report Sweden, 2020). Thus, the pandemic strategy adopted in Sweden differed significantly from the steps taken in other EU countries. Sweden justified its liberal approach by the need to develop herd immunity to combat the pandemic. It was more in the nature of a recommendation and suggestion and aimed to induce the development of natural population immunity.

For the other 27 countries, the government policy was significantly more restrictive in nature. None of the countries replicated the Swedish model based on building population resilience (the United Kingdom initially aimed to do so, although this policy was later abandoned). As already noted, these countries have achieved a score that describes their policies as restrictive. However, the significant dispersion for the score in this group for the GPCI is between 19 and 25, allowing us to look at the results by creating an internal typology to represent their specificity, by distinguishing significantly restrictive policies and moderately restrictive policies. The former type of country includes 18 countries (Austria, Belgium, Bulgaria, Republic of Cyprus, the Czech Republic, Estonia, France, Greece, Hungary, Ireland, Italy, Latvia, Malta, Poland, Portugal, Romania, Slovakia, and Spain); the latter, only 9 countries (Croatia, Denmark, Finland, Germany, Lithuania,

Luxembourg, the Netherlands, Slovenia, the United Kingdom). Countries with moderately restrictive policies did not undertake significant tightening on some instruments. For example, the wearing of masks was either recommended or only in enclosed spaces where it was not possible to keep a distance. Thus, although their policies are considered restrictive, there were signs of liberal solutions.

The concept of social capital provides some explanation of social reality. It looks for the cause of uneven development of societies. It also allows answering the question of how a society will behave in a crisis situation, including during a pandemic.

Although, as a research concept, it is not yet elaborated or unambiguous, especially in the area of methodology, on the basis of the analysis some conclusions can be drawn about the problem studied:

First, the study showed disparities between countries in terms of social capital. The countries, which are so-called new EU members, i.e. those that joined the EU after 2004, show less social capital. One can emphasise the unique character of the organisation, in which the functioning contributes not only to economic changes but also to social changes – including common norms and values.

Second, the analysis conducted allowed us to confirm three of the four hypotheses regarding the relationship between social capital and effective management during a pandemic, including:

H2 – as social capital increases in a country, there is a reduction in the negative effects of the pandemic in terms of reduced hospitalisations for COVID-19;

H3 – with an increase in social capital in a country, there is an increase in the vaccination of the population against COVID-19;

H4 – as social capital increases in a country, there is a reduction in the negative effects of the pandemic in terms of reduced mortality.

The most important determinant of effectiveness during a pandemic is the reduction in mortality. The highest correlation was between social capital and mortality. Global mortality data show that the pandemic hit the Americas and Europe particularly hard. Peru has the highest COVID-19 mortality rate in the world, with 615 deaths per 100,000 people. Bosnia and Herzegovina, Northern Macedonia, Montenegro, Bulgaria, and Hungary have the next highest mortality rates, each with more than 300 deaths per 100,000 people. Bulgaria and Hungary are the countries with the lowest social capital. It is important to keep in mind that the actual number of deaths due to COVID-19 is much higher because in many countries the number of excess deaths exceeds the number of deaths due to coronavirus as evidenced by insufficient testing in many countries. Moreover, the official result does not take into account the enormous collateral damage caused by COVID-19. Around the world, patients fail to find medical care for other conditions due to the limited availability of medical facilities. They also avoid seeking care for fear of getting infected. These are additional aspects that may further confirm the correlation results obtained in the study.

Finally, it is worth mentioning the limitations of the present study. One is that it was difficult to compare social capital in the pre-pandemic period. Complete data for 2021 were simply not yet available. It might be interesting here to compare the first and second waves of the pandemic when there was no vaccine on the market (year 2020) with the third and fourth waves when EU communities had vaccine protection available. Due to the fact that the study covered only countries belonging to the EU, the assumption cannot be generalised and applicable to all countries in the world. It should be remembered that within the EU there is a single market, including freedom of movement, which affects the spread of the COVID-19. In addition, the EU is united by common values, including respect for the law, community of norms, and Christian tradition. These values indicate a fairly high level of social capital. Thus, they do not allow generalising how the situation will look in countries with low social capital.

Since vaccines for coronavirus became available in late 2020, they have prevented countless hospitalisations and deaths. But many countries have not yet achieved sufficient vaccination coverage, leaving millions of people vulnerable to severe illness due to COVID-19.

The impact of COVID-19 on the economy of the EU has been even harder than due to the global financial crisis. The EU economy has suffered a large recession in 2020 due to stricter measures and lockdowns that have contributed to high output swathes of economic activity, decline in private consumption and increase in household savings. Public finances took a considerable hit as a result of the severe recession and the necessary policy response, with increased fiscal divergence between Member States. The EU response to the crisis was carried out in a coordinated manner.

Considering sectoral impacts, services have been most affected. The first wave of pandemic led to a decrease in employment, drop in demand, and production losses in almost all manufacturing industries; disruptions in global supply chains due to closure of factories in Europe and China; and additional costs due to intensified health and security measures. The second wave seems to have been less harmful. Pharmaceutical production and production of computers and other devices have been affected the least. Other manufacturing industries have been hit relatively hard during the first wave and undertook a path towards recovery during the second wave of pandemic.

Obtained results in Chapter 3 also confirm outcomes of Chapter 1 concerning strictness of "lockdown style" policies and quite similar level of restrictions provided by EU states. In the majority of the EU states, a stricter response of government policies has gone in line with growing level of economic support. The level of restrictions negatively correlates with Economic Sentiment and Confidence Indicators (i.e. industrial, services, retail trade, construction, and consumer confidence) in all EU countries. In some of them, we can observe a highly strong negative dependence. Moreover, unemployment expectations over the next 12 months highly depend on restriction measures. So, we can conclude that the confidence in the economy of EU citizens has largely depended on the implemented restrictions.

In terms of the Economic Support Index, the highest average level is in Cyprus (100), Ireland (98.42), the United Kingdom (96.05), Austria (94.45) and Slovak Republic (91.24), while the lowest in Germany (41.28), Sweden (48.98), Hungary (49.94), Croatia (55.67), France (58.02), and Estonia (59.71). In some EU states (i.e. Austria, Spain, Finland, Greece, Italy, Lithuania, Poland, and Slovak Republic), confidence in the economy of EU citizens highly depends on such measures as income support, debt relief for households, and fiscal measures.

In recent days, Europe prepares for the fourth wave of pandemic and is divided between countries which have imposed COVID-19 restrictions on unvaccinated citizens (like Germany, Austria, and Slovakia) and those which have not (like France and Poland). On the one hand, strict public health measures could lead to wider social and economic crises. On the other hand, assuming a situation where the vaccine is effective but governments focus on keeping the economy open, thus consumer confidence fades, and these initiatives however fail. In our opinion, even in the case of partially effective vaccine, transparent and evidence-based communication, citizens' active engagement and cooperation with the government can lead to protective immunity in the population.

Scenarios regarding how the economy of EU States will recover after the current shock will depend on the way the pandemic will end. There are two perspectives – the pandemic will subside either rapidly (as in the case of Spanish flu) or gradually, over a longer period. The success in fighting coronavirus and its consequences, which include economic stagnation, depends on effectiveness of the government policy, the capacity of States and their healthcare systems in time of crisis and the society's willingness to adhere to emergency rules.

Among the key recommendations on the recovery measures and policies are the following: to develop the competitiveness of the EU industry via investments in R&D and digital re/upskilling; to increase cross-country collaboration in innovative industrial projects, including healthcare; to improve productive specialisation of poorer regions; to reduce the high and divergent public debt ratios in a sustainable, growth-friendly manner; to reinforce counter-cyclicality in the EU fiscal framework; to foster public and private investment; to prevent and correct macroeconomic imbalances; and to ensure transparent and evidence-based communication between government and citizens as well as coordination at the EU level.

Index